Gold Experience

Also by Jim Walsh
Published by the University of Minnesota Press

Bar Yarns and Manic-Depressive Mixtapes:
Jim Walsh on Music from Minneapolis to the Outer Limits

GOLD

EXPERIENCE

Following Prince in the '90s

Jim Walsh

University of Minnesota Press

Minneapolis

London

Published by the University of Minnesota Press
111 Third Avenue South, Suite 290
Minneapolis, MN 55401-2520
http://www.upress.umn.edu

ISBN 978-1-5179-0258-2

A Cataloging-in-Publication record for this book is available from the Library of Congress.

Printed in the United States of America on acid-free paper

The University of Minnesota is an equal-opportunity educator and employer.

23 22 21 20 19 18 17   10 9 8 7 6 5 4 3 2 1

Contents

1996

1997

1998

1999

2000–2002

Introduction

PRINCE AND I BOTH LOVE MUSIC AND BASKETBALL, SO it's only fitting that I found out that the little love god had passed away as my son Henry and I were on our way to our twice-weekly basketball game, Thursday, April 21, 2016, 11:50 A.M.

Jade Tittle, somber and far away, broke the news to us via The Current (89.3), Minnesota Public Radio's influential alternative music station that in the last decade of his life became the go-to source for all things Prince. I say "far away" because the volume was down on the car radio, but even from a distance I could hear the gravity in the deejay's voice. The disbelief.

Shit.

No.

I turned it up. With great deliberation and palpable shock, Jade confirmed that a body had been found at Paisley Park, and that it had been identified as Prince, age fifty-seven. We were at Forty-sixth and Grand Avenue in South Minneapolis. I stared at the stenciled letters on the door of Kings Wine Bar and at the red stop sign in front of us. I patted my son on his basketball shorts, turned the car around, and said, "Dude, I gotta work."

He slumped into a respectful silence, and we drove somberly back to my home office as Prince's music filled the car and memories of his life flashed before me, including the last time I saw him, at Paisley Park for his January 21, 2016, Piano and a Microphone solo show. I went as a guest of my friend Andrea Swensson, whose thoughtful, passionate, and playful coverage of Prince over the past few years for The Current kept me in touch with the latter-day doings of this brilliant artist I covered in the '90s, when I was the pop music critic at the *St. Paul Pioneer Press*. The show was fantastic, of course, one I'd always dreamed of seeing Prince stage, and a few weeks later I wrote a short blurb about it for the Minneapolis-based *Star Tribune*:

> Sitting at his purple piano, hair and fingers flying amid the grandeur of a kaleidoscope light show, the Beautiful One made like his one-time muse Wolfgang Amadeus Mozart in as memorable a one-man performance of music as I've ever had the pleasure of witnessing. Bravo and more, please.

Now here he was, just a few weeks later, dead. No more. The void was instant and as unfathomable to me then as it is now at the moment of this writing. As Prince's body lay in an elevator at his Paisley Park compound in Chanhassen, his magnificent heart having stopped from what the Midwest Medical Examiner's office in Ramsey would weeks later deem to be "a self-administered deadly dose of the synthetic opiate fentanyl," the planet sobbed and a rainbow appeared in the skies over Paisley.

"This is what it sounds like when the whole world weeps," I posted on Facebook and Twitter, then returned a phone call from my editor at Minnpost.com and wrote a fast eulogy.

THAT NIGHT I went to the Mad Ripple Hootenanny, the ten-year-old singer/songwriter showcase I host and play at in Minneapolis whose weekly meetings can sometimes feel like a drunken church. This night it was all that and more, and thanks to my buddies Shawn Stelton and Doug Collins we were able to open and close the night with mournful versions of "Purple Rain" and a handful of other Prince tunes. At the same time, the entire universe erupted in Prince music, with previously unseen videos and unheard tracks from the vault being shared like newly unearthed scriptures, and in downtown Minneapolis outside First Avenue an impromptu service and tribute got blasted out via social media and The Current.

For the rest of the weekend I went fetal, mainlining Prince's music, writing, weeping, and finally that Sunday night, as so often happens with sudden death, I felt a need to gather up everything I could find in my fan's archives and hold it close. I pulled together all my Prince vinyl, CDs, cassettes, bootlegs, and newspaper clippings, and I spent the night reading articles and liner notes.

I went through the boxes, some of which I hadn't touched since the '90s, and I was happy to discover I had saved some good stuff: press releases for all sorts of events, including the Valentine's Day 1994 release of "The Most Beautiful Girl in the World" single. Magazines, including copies of the old *Controversy* fanzine, Neal Karlen's *Rolling Stone* cover story, various Prince-related *Village Voice* Pazz and Jop polls, and cover stories from *Vibe, Jet, Billboard,* and *SPIN.*

Catalogs from the old New Power Generation retail store in Uptown. A short-lived CD-ROM experience called ♀ *Interactive* and the floppy disc with the software to translate the Prince symbol into newsprint. The notebook and pencil I used to interview him, and hard copies of my three interviews with him. Napkins from the *Emancipation* CD release party and a napkin from the 1996 Prince–Mayte wedding reception, fashioned for the one-night-only bash with a combo *M* and ♀. A small box of his favorite cereal, Cap'n Crunch, bowlfuls of which he provided to guests at his pajama parties. A press laminate from the 1994 NBA All-Star Game party at Paisley Park, probably the most star-studded night in the studio's history. A beautiful booklet/program from 1995 with my liner notes from *The Gold Experience* that I never knew existed; a cool one-sheet for the "Rock 'n' Roll Is Alive (and It Lives in Minneapolis)" single; and a very cool note he sent to me around Christmastime in the late '90s that read "Peace and be wild."

A FEW WEEKS LATER, I started digging around some more, and this book is what I found. What follows is a real-time version of my coverage for the *Pioneer Press* from 1994 to 2002. None of these news clips are readily available online, so I had to buy all the transcripts of my stories from newslibrary.com and reproduce them here with permission from the *St. Paul Pioneer Press*.

Rereading them today, it's clear I was always rooting for Prince, or defending him, and I wasn't alone. Countless Prince record reviews over the years concluded with the stunningly unoriginal thesis that a specific record or concert was a return to his '80s glory days, so it's perfect that in the weeks after his death it was Prince—staunch defender of the independent recording artist and foe of the record industry—who became the first artist in the history of the *Billboard* 200 album chart to land five titles simultaneously in the Top 10.

In 1997, before his *Jam of the Year* tour landed at Target Center, I asked ♀ via fax if he thought people were starved for the real spontaneity and fan–musician connection he provides. "They're definitely starved," he replied, "and ● am the chef!"

Bon appétit. For me, it was always an honor, pleasure, and great joy to cover, interview, spar with, and bear witness to the genius of Prince, or the Artist Formerly Known as Prince, or the Artist, or ♀ as he was known for the bulk of the time I wrote and reported about him. I started working at the *Pioneer Press* in September 1994; I began writing about Prince that February and kept at it for almost ten years. He was a beat unto himself: I wrote about him for *Billboard, Melody Maker, Newsday* and continued writing about him occasionally after I left the *Pioneer Press* in 2003. I never lost track of him or stopped listening to him.

I ALWAYS FELT LIKE I WAS WRITING a history book when I was covering Prince; this is it. Frankly, I scrambled to put this book together because his and other deaths of late make me believe that time is of the essence and that these writings can help flesh out a little-reported time in Prince's career. I also wanted to put it together because I miss the man and his music, and the written word has always helped me make sense of life and loss.

When Prince was alive, there was a comforting feeling around these parts, knowing that hot flame was out in his mad scientist laboratory in Chanhassen, burning bright. Now that it's been snuffed out, I want to preserve what I can while I can.

Thanks to Erik Anderson and everybody at the University of Minnesota Press for making this book happen so well and so fast. Thanks to my agent, Michael Croy of Northstar Literary Agency, for his support and encouragement. Thanks to Amy Nelson at the *Pioneer Press* for giving us the green light, and to all my former *PiPress* colleagues, especially fellow Prince reporters/fans Chris Hewitt, Bruce Orwall, and Amy Carlson Gustafson, and to my *Pioneer Press* editors in the '90s: Pat Mc-Morrow, Jim Tarbox, Sue Campbell, Don Boxmeyer, Larry May, Bob Shaw, Ken Doctor, Walker Lundy, and especially Dana Davis, who wrote many of the headlines you're about to read.

And thanks always to Prince, for all the dead-not-dead music and magic.

Peace and be wild.

1994

Prince's Magic Lures the Stars

MAGIC JOHNSON STOOD WITH HIS WIFE, COOKIE, IN THE back of the soundstage room at Paisley Park Studios, rocking to the bass-heavy mix being pumped out by the house deejay. It was 2 A.M. Sunday, but Johnson's eyes were as big as any Prince fan's eyes can get. "I don't care how late it gets. I'm not leaving until he leaves the stage," the former NBA great said over the deafening sound of the booming speakers. "He's the best. A genius. I love everything he does, but my wife and I especially like his ballads."

Magic and Cookie should be in seventh heaven on this Valentine's Day, then, because one of Prince's finest-ever pop ballads, "The Most Beautiful Girl in the World," hits stores today. Johnson was one of six hundred or so guests at an early-morning invite-only party Prince threw at Paisley Park Sunday to commemorate the release of "Beautiful Girl," an exquisitely down-to-earth torch song that celebrates the power of womankind.

At midnight, visitors began arriving at Paisley Park, which was decked out in a lavish Roman Empire-meets-cyberspace motif that went by the name of "The Beautiful Experience." The guests included NBA players David Robinson, Clyde Drexler, Dominique Wilkins, Alonzo Mourning, Danny Manning, Dikembe Mutombo, and James Jackson; Vikings wide receiver Cris Carter; television stars Will Smith, Downtown Julie Brown, Daisy Fuentes, and Bill Bellamy; hip-hop kids Kriss Kross; soul-singing phenom Tevin Campbell; members of pop music groups Salt-N-Pepa, Soul Asylum, and the Gin Blossoms; and—get this—power-of-positive-thinking dude Tony Robbins.

They sauntered from room to room, taking in a jazz quintet led by saxophonist Eric Leeds, videos in a mini-theater space, and a PG-rated peep show, where they could check out live, if lame, sex on stage.

But beyond the surreal schmoozathon aspect, the all-night bash served as a coming-out party and promotional vehicle for "Beautiful Girl." The video for the song makes its world premiere on MTV today, but partygoers were treated to a sneak preview of the clip, which depicts women of all shapes, sizes, and colors in various roles/fantasies—from childbirth to beauty contests to a black woman as Forty-third President of the United States. The night was filled with video images, pictures, and posters of Prince. Finally, at 3:15, the real thing—clad in black and sporting fishhook-shaped sideburns and an Artful Dodger top hat—hit the stage with his new five-piece band and dancer Mayte in tow.

The scintillating nine-song performance consisted of all new material, much of which was hard blues–flecked rock and spare guitar-driven funk songs that follow the lead of "Beautiful Girl" by taking to task sexist rappers and attempting a redefinition of the beauty myth. Throughout the seventy-minute set (which was videotaped for future release), Prince appeared to be loose and genuinely having fun. But there was a purpose to the material that has been missing in recent years.

On the opening number ("Days of Wild"?), he howled, "Call her 'bitch or ho' / I don't think so. . . . A woman should be thanked every day." There was a sinewy blues ballad, "We Got to Break It Down," which appeared to speak to the hardships of keeping a long-term relationship afloat. And at one point, over a wicked guitar line, he proclaimed, "It's 1994 / Don't worry about the name. . . . There was 'Irresistible Bitch' and 'Sexy MF' / That was then, this is now."

Clearly, Prince has matured when it comes to matters of the heart and matters of the female, though—make no mistake— all of it is filtered through his own inimitable brand of sexuality-slash-mysticism. And if Sunday morning's performance is any indication, he's poised to record his most thoughtful and meaningful music since 1987's *Sign o' the Times* album. ■

He's Not Just Another Pretty Symbol

February 18

AROUND THE TIME *PURPLE RAIN* CAME OUT IN 1984, THERE was a story going around the Twin Cities that Prince was showing up at the Southtown movie theater, sitting in the back row night after night taking in multiple viewings of *Amadeus*. Even if it's not true, it's a great story: I love the image of Prince alone in the back row of a dark movie house, his album and movie No. 1 in the country, gleaning solace and inspiration from another composer who turned the world on its ear two centuries prior.

It's lonely at the top, Tom Hulce as Mozart would say to the new purple boy genius. *That's me,* Prince would say back to the screen and himself, slinking out of the theater before the end credits and crowd started rolling.

For some reason, the *Amadeus* story was the first thing I thought of when Prince changed his name to a symbol last summer. Maybe I should have listened to those wise and rocking anchorpeople and gossip columnists when their thirteen-second "Isn't this guy a weirdo?" stories came out, thus saving me the embarrassment of this confession. But I didn't. Instead, I wondered.

And now I wonder aloud. Just what if Prince adopted the symbol not as a publicity stunt but as a way of reclaiming himself, as an attempt to elevate his gift, his genius beyond words and a culture that makes mincemeat out of gifts and genius?

Back then, I felt a little silly about my theory. But since *The Hits/The B Sides* came out, I'm convinced that I, and he, was right all along. And after watching his performance last Sunday morning at Paisley Park, I'm more convinced than ever.

One incident in particular made me think back to the *Amadeus* legend. To say the least, it was a surreal night: dry ice and pseudo-bacchanalian theme rooms and basketball players and rock stars and scantily clad, feather-draped women performing spontaneous dances ("Like never-never land with little girls instead of little boys," observed Soul Asylum manager Bill Sullivan). But all that became so much perfunctory window dressing when Prince hit the stage at 3:15 A.M.

After running through a batch of new material with his band (keyboardists Tommy Barbarella and Mr. Hayes, drummer Michael Bland, bassist Sonny T.), a little-known guest guitarist took the stage. Prince was seated at a pristine white piano with the word *Beautiful* inscribed on the side and was riffing on the opening boogie-woogie run to Ray Charles's "What'd I Say." The kid stood center stage, fumbling with his guitar and pedals, until he finally gave up and traipsed over to the piano bench. He bent down and talked for about twenty seconds into Prince's stony ear.

But unbeknownst to the kid, he wasn't at Paisley Park anymore. In the blink of an eye, Prince had become Mozart and the kid Salieri, "the patron saint of mediocrity." And he was about to become an unwitting player in a postmodern restaging of the scene in *Amadeus* when Mozart plays a composition while hanging upside down, then humiliates Salieri with a lampooning of the other composer's own work.

Grudgingly, Prince got up from the piano as the band chugged along behind him. He picked up the kid's guitar, briefly inspected it, then strapped it on. The kid stood behind Prince with his hands on his hips and nervously puffed at his bangs. With no effort at all, Prince placed his hands on the instrument and made it come to life—first with a slow, bending riff, then with a muscular, out-of-this world lead. Sixty seconds was all. He stopped, handed the guitar back to the kid, and said into the mike, "I just wanted to see if it worked." The crowd went berserk with laughter.

He returned to the piano and, behind the kid's back, exaggeratedly rolled his eyes. More laughter. The band continued to crank, and the kid did his best to recover by pumping out some ordinary Chuck Berry riffs. But the damage had been done. Compared with Prince's fireworks, the guitar was returned to its original state as a hunk of metal, wood, and strings, not a magic wand. It was, in the words of another Minnesota Mozart, "a guitar in the hands of a man who just can't play." When the song came to an end, Prince introduced "Bud Lite on guitar" and graciously implored the crowd to "Give it up, give it up" for the kid. Then under his breath but clearly into the mike, he said, "Give it up. And he should."

Give or take Isaiah Rider's "East Bay Funk," it was the best slam of the weekend.

In that instant, Prince showed why he's head and shoulders above most any and all who call themselves musicians these days. Call it what you will: a competitive mean streak or an obsessive desire to be the best. But whatever makes a genius a genius, Prince has got it in spades.

But his dis of the kid wasn't even the high point of the morning. That came in waves as he unveiled his new original material, a stripped-down *Dirty Mind* meets *Sign o' the Times* stew that took to task his old sexist ways and made for an exhilarating fast-forward/postfeminist feel. But the evolution didn't hatch itself in a vacuum: during a break in the action Sunday morning, Prince's publicist, Karen Lee, took to the stage to explain the genesis of his latest single, "The Most Beautiful Girl in the World." In response to Paisley's personal ads from an "eligible bachelor" who was seeking "the most beautiful girl in the world," Lee explained, Paisley had received more than fifty thousand responses from women of all walks of life who define beauty in myriad ways. It may not have been exactly the reaction Prince was looking for, but in a weird way it has obviously served as an outreach for an artist who has too often had his head in the sand/Batcave. The letter writers became, in a sense, collaborators.

At various points in his career, Prince has appeared to be cooked or kooky, but take it from a newly won-over re-believer: Sunday morning's wee-hour set proved that the guy is about to reinvent himself. Again. And if you're skeptical of that report, I guess I don't blame you. But if you'd seen the unlikely trio of Dikembe Mutombo, Tony Robbins, and Danny Manning all up near the front of the stage swaying together at four in the morning last weekend, you'd believe that something special was going on, too. Because then you would have heard it. You would have heard it when Dikembe, Tony, and Danny led the crowd of basketball players, rock stars, and guests in a silent chant: "Rock me, Amadeus." ∎

Prince Treats Lucky Fans to After-hours Rehearsal

May 26

A S PART OF GLAM SLAM'S ONGOING EROTIC CITY AFTER-hours party, Prince and his band showed up at 2 A.M. Wednesday to turn in a laid-back, five-song, forty-minute jam in front of 150 fans. As far as polished performances go, the set was fairly unremarkable—save for a couple of spellbinding solos by electric violinist Denis Boder of the Los Angeles band Floor 13 and some typically great guitar fireworks from Prince—but the show provided late-night club crawlers a sneak peak at a band rehearsal, complete with Prince counting off parts, making up arrangements on the spot, and running the soundboard.

Kicking off the jam with a slow blues burn, Prince lay on his back for the first two songs and picked out feathery leads while band members took turns at solos. The highlight of the night was a version of Sly & the Family Stone's "I Want to Take You Higher," featuring Prince on bass. After performing "Get Wild," a new original penned by bassist Sonny Thompson, Prince ended the night by saying, "Come back tomorrow, y'all, and we'll make a big noise."

At press time Wednesday, the rumor was that Prince was organizing a scavenger hunt for all denizens of Thursday morning's edition of Erotic City, the prize for which was said to be tickets to a private concert at Paisley Park Studios, where the Adrenalized One has reportedly been itching to break in a new stage dubbed "The Endorphin Machine." ∎

Prince's "Big Noise" for Fans at His House Doesn't Disappoint

May 27

"COME BACK TOMORROW, AND WE'LL MAKE A BIG NOISE," Prince told a crowd of 150 nightcrawlers at the end of an unannounced forty-minute jam at Glam Slam's after-hours Erotic City club Tuesday night/Wednesday morning. Come back they did, and Prince kept his promise.

After the clubs closed Wednesday, some 350 arrivees to Glam Slam paid $10 to get into Erotic City and were met by an exotic dancer/bingo caller who led them through the paces of a Prince-styled scavenger hunt. Participants were instructed to perform three tasks: write down the chorus of Prince's latest hit, "The Most Beautiful Girl in the World"; write down the names of two of Prince's band members; and collect a guitar pick sticker from one of the several dancers who were roaming the Erotic City pedestals.

The fans joined in on the freaky festivities and after turning in their booty to the Erotic City staff were issued a ticket to an after-hours bash at Paisley Park Studios in Chanhassen. Upon arrival, the crowd was escorted into the Paisley soundstage, where Prince's new stage, a gigantic futuristic contraption dubbed "The Endorphin Machine," was bathed in fog and awash in multicolored backlights.

At 3 A.M., the band (keyboardists Tommy Barbarella and Mr. Hayes, bassist Sonny T., drummer Michael Bland, and cameo violinist Denis Boder) mounted the stage, and Prince asked the congregation, "You like my house?" The comment was met with a smattering of squeals, and as the band eased into a slow, sultry version of "The Most Beautiful Girl in the World," a group of female fans called out, "We want a beautiful experience!" At that, the singer, clad in crushed red velvet, slunk behind the curtains of the stage's main compartment, which looked to house a fully equipped bedroom. With a cordless microphone, he dared the women to come back so he could make good on their request. A few cautiously approached the compartment but promptly jumped back when they drew back the curtain and came face to face with the little love god himself.

The first hour of the set showcased Prince's customary (ho-hum) guitar wizardry. On the third song of the night, he used the hard blues foundation of a new number, "Race," to fire off a variety of muscular, expressive, jaw-dropping leads in which not a note was wasted. It was the most astonishing display of rock-guitar virtuosity I have ever witnessed in concert, a performance that reinforces the idea that when it comes to greatness, there are only a couple of rock guitarists in Prince's league. And they're dead.

Other standouts of the first set were "Shhh" (a song written for Tevin Campbell that appeared on Campbell's last album) and "Get Wild," a new party rave written by Sonny T. "We ain't got no curfew in my house," Prince told the crowd as the clock approached 4 A.M. Then, over the campily clichéd sound of a deejay scratching vinyl, he asked, "You all want it live?"

The band lurched into "Days of Wild," an exhilarating funk-rocker that lyrically and musically pits the transient nature of hip-hop with the musical chops of an old-school genius. When he intoned, "I can tear shit up, that's my style," the message was clear: hip-hop may be the most commercially successful and influential music of the moment, but most of those sucker emcees couldn't run with Prince on a real musical instrument if their entire collection of James Brown vinyl depended on it. Prince played the song with such fury, such purposefulness, such playfulness that he broke a string on his bass. Still, he continued playing for a good ten minutes, pounding out defiant slaps and leads, refusing to let go of the groove that had possessed his bad self.

After a fifteen-minute break, it was almost as if a different band had entered the Endorphin Machine. If the first set highlighted Prince's newfound love affair with the guitar, the second emphasized his ongoing love affair with R&B. The set opened with the soul workout "Acknowledge Me," which he performed on *Soul Train* last week. After a couple more hard R&B tunes, the night ended with the lights all the way down for "Dark," a dense, synthesized, horn-punctuated ballad that Prince introduced as "a song about loneliness" and sang like the kid cousin of Al Green.

At one point, Prince said, "Ain't no party like a New Power party," in reference to his loyal fan club, the New Power Generation, many members of which were in attendance. As the moon hung in the sky over Chanhassen at 4:45 Thursday morning, the sun was just starting to come up. Inside, Prince grinned graciously at the crowd of weary but delirious scavenger hunters. "You can't thank me as much as I can thank you," he said over the fading organ waves of "Dark."

"Come back anytime. It's your house, too." ■

Best of May

IT WAS MAY, MAY, THAT LUSTY MONTH OF MAY, AND FROM the virgin voyage of REV 105 to Prince's late-night jams at Glam Slam's new after-hours club, Erotic City, there were more than a few affairs to remember.

Prince, Erotic City (various late nights/early mornings, Glam Slam's second level). One night, he assembles a full-blown horn section and ringleads an old-style jam that evokes a postmodern Cotton Club. One night, the jazz vibe is so cool you'd swear the joint was the Village Vanguard. The next, he lays on his back playing lazy, lightning leads that make it feel like the Blue Note. One night, he invites an electric violinist to create a Hendrix-gypsy vibe; the next, he Pied-Pipers the entire club out to Paisley Park to perform a full-fledged concert. One night, there are forty people. The next, four hundred. One night, he barely talks or sings. The next, he's loose as a funky goose.

Creatively and clubwise, this is easily the most exciting—and most visible—period the twin towns have seen from the little big man in a decade. And if you can get past the fun-but-forced "erotic" atmosphere and some of the power-tripping bouncers, these are intimate, intoxicating shows you'll tell your grandkids about. Because if the summer of '84 was the summer of *Purple Rain*, then the summer of '94 is shaping up to be the summer of Erotic City. So get out the extra-strength coffee and the toothpicks for your eyelids. Like the song says, "These are the days of wild." ■

Best of July

CIRCLE THE DRAIN (UPTOWN BAR, JULY 25). A RECENT *New York Times* article on America's hottest music scenes included a dispatch from Chicago, which griped about the backbiting that exists in the Windy City and claimed that there is little cooperation or cross-pollination within cliques/ bands/camps. Well, for my money, spontaneous hootenannies like this one—the absolute antithesis of all that one-upmanship nonsense—epitomize the long-held ethic that players from around these parts love to play. For all concerned, it is one of those beautiful things that never registers on the official quality-of-life polls but almost makes up for indoor major league baseball and January.

As Prince kicked it downtown, this all-star group of local rock luminaries, including members of Soul Asylum, the Jayhawks, Uncle Tupelo/Wilco, and Run Westy Run, stayed uptown and whipped up one of the funnest country and rock jamborees in recent memory. Far too many highlights to mention, but . . . Gary Louris lent his sweet soul tenor to the opening number, a raggedly glorious reading of Rosanne Cash's "Seven Year Ache." Danny Murphy tore through an impassioned version of The Clash's "Stay Free." Jeff Tweedy unveiled a magical bit of melancholia titled "Passenger Seat." Kraig Johnson's miniset included knee-buckling takes on the Stones' "Long Cold Winter" and Vic Chesnutt's "Where Were You When I Needed You?" In between, there were songs by Roger Miller, Tom Petty, and more than a few spine chills.

PRINCE AND THE NEW POWER GENERATION (Glam Slam, July 26). To talk about this gig, you have to go back to a show at Glam Slam in February '93. That night, Prince played a three-set marathon, a greatest-hits revue delivered with dollops of spirit and showmanship. To a man, it was admittedly pretty mind-boggling to hear all those monster hits in one sitting. But underneath it, I got the uneasy feeling that the stuff was just this side of stale. That was one impression, and there were two others: that Prince was bored out of his skull and that he was purging himself of his past.

The memory of that '93 gig was stapled in my craw as I stood on the floor with a few hundred other gyrating gland slammers who took in this, the second installment of Prince's two-night benefit for the National Kidney Foundation. Throughout the summer, Prince has quietly served notice to after-hours denizens of Erotic City that there is a musical reason for the name-to-symbol change: Prince was then, and ♀ is now. And last Tuesday night, 1,200 people got the message, too, in a concert that relied exclusively on new material and reestablished him as (forget the gossip columnists, your Prince-dissin' friends, and your own well-deserved, well-entrenched reservations) the preeminent live performer of our time.

Over the two-hour set, His Former Royal Badness was anything but his old enigmatic self; instead, he was loose, passionate, campy, self-deprecating, and playful. With dancer/vocalist Mayte as his foil/partner in erotic crime, he staged an impromptu fashion show with a series of Dr. Seuss–styled hats, cajoled/flirted with the audience, and pledged his allegiance to his childhood hero-turned-NPG bass player Sonny Thompson. But along with the funky frivolity, there was also a serious theme to the evening: women and children first.

After opening with the dazzling power ballad "Gold," P and NPG settled into a groove that folded in his missives neatly, effortlessly. During the anti-gun rave-up "Love Sign," Mayte held up placards that spoke to the importance of kids and education. On "Papa," a sinewy rocker about child abuse, the androgynous little superfreak gave voice to the Moral Majority's worst nightmare: "Don't abuse your children, or they'll turn out like me." On the partial reading of "Days of Wild," he warned, "Call her a 'bitch' or 'ho,' I don't think so," and the prerecorded rap "Pussy Power'" was neither as sexist nor as obvious as its title, but a bawdy paean to motherhood and the organic strength of female sexuality. (Given all this femme worship, it's no wonder that, as one concertgoer pointed out, Prince's new stage, the Endorphin Machine, resembles the outline of a vagina.)

Minneapolis music intelligentsia will tell you that Prince's finest club moment came in 1981, when he stormed First Avenue for a nasty jam the night after the *Controversy* concert at Met Center. But after last week, it may be time to rewrite the history books. For as Tuesday's show proved, Prince-slash-♀ is navigating what is arguably the most interesting musical period of his career. At Monday night's gig, somebody shouted out a request for "Free Bird." A ridiculous request, to be sure, but at this point, the only thing more ridiculous would be a request for "Purple Rain." ∎

My sister Molly was my date for this show. I'd been at the Uptown Bar seeing Circle the Drain *(later Golden Smog), and when I hit the door at Glam Slam, the band wasn't onstage. Prince's manager at the time told me he'd been waiting for me, saying, "I'm not going on until Jim Walsh is here." This was the first inkling I'd had that he'd read anything I'd written. After the show, his manager fetched me and said Prince wanted to meet me. Molly and I went up to the second-floor backstage area at Glam Slam, where I was introduced to Prince for the first time. He had a warm postgig glow and wanted to know what I thought of the show. I raved, and he thanked me for writing about him and then softly said he thought we could collaborate on a project together. I wasn't sure what he meant, so I said, "That sounds like a book. I'd love to write that book." In the end he was talking about the liner notes to* The Gold Experience *and, yes, this book.*

Songs in the Key of Life

August 16

IN PREDICTABLY CRYPTIC FASHION, THE ARTWORK ON Prince's new album *Come* features a funeral motif, complete with the deceased's time on earth: "1958–1993." Obviously, this tombstone-worthy testimonial refers to Prince's metamorphosis into ♀. But for the critically embattled genius, *Come* is more of a rebirth than a death.

Throughout his career, Prince has been cast as a musical prodigy, love nymph, quasi-religious icon, and out-of-touch space cadet—and has made some truly terrible records. But while the damage to his public image may have led many to write him off as old news, *Come* is a breakthrough. It reveals a guise of the guy who has been all but forgotten: a human being. On "Letitgo," the album's first single, Prince sings low, easy, and autobiographically: "All my life I've kept my feelings deep inside, I never was a person to let somebody know. . . . Now I gotta let it go and let my feelings show."

This reawakening has manifested itself in much of ♀'s most recent material, most notably his last two singles. "The Most Beautiful Girl in the World" bent over backward to damage-control Prince's history of treating women as sex toys/goddesses, while "Love Sign," his duet with Nona Gaye, is a sweet funk-pop jam about kids and guns that asks, "If you only had one year left to live, what good is the time you spend if you got no love to give?" Which is to speculate that at thirty-six Prince's larger sense of responsibility is kicking in like never before. (Recent live shows have included a cover of Sly Stone's "Babies Makin' Babies.") While his 1987 album *Sign o' the Times* traversed similar political terrain, *Come* is a more personally political work, the centerpiece of which is the remarkable "Papa," a smoldering blues-framed number about child abuse.

(In his 1992 composition "The Sacrifice of Victor," Prince frankly writes about his childhood. Epileptic until the age of seven, he says he acquired a somewhat fatalistic worldview. Even more candidly than on "Papa," he relays a hard-won tale of abuse: "Mama held up her baby for protection, from a man with a strap in his hand. I remember what I want.")

But "Papa" isn't a cry for sympathy; it's catharsis. "There's always a rainbow at the end of every rain," he concludes and, like anyone else approaching middle age, suggests that he's starting to look back while pushing forward. Fiercefully. Now more than ever before, Prince seems committed to making meaningful work. Most important, it's got a nice beat, and you can dance to it.

The bigot-bashing "Race" is a tightly delivered dance blow-out that never slips into touchy-feely rhetoric, and the wildly romantic ballad "Dark" is a playful paean to the joys of lovemaking. Then there's the exquisite string-swaddled "Solo," cowritten by *M. Butterfly* composer David Henry Hwang, which confronts the singer's fear of self-imposed solitary confinement.

"I'm so tired of being alone." Al Green said that, but on much of *Come*, Prince implies it over and over again, as if he genuinely wants to connect—with you, me, himself, his band, the world at large. And while he has historically crusaded for utopian community ("Uptown," "1999," "Days of Wild") and collaboration ("Graffiti Bridge," "Paisley Park," "2 Nigs United 4 West Compton"), such songs have more often than not been sprinkled with Oz-like fairy dust.

Therein, as is always the case with Prince, lies the paradox. The promotional copy for *Come* reads, "This is the dawning of a new spiritual revolution." Well, call me a New Power Generation heretic, but no, it's not. This is the release of an excellent new album, period, and the moments that resonate deepest off *Come* are the ones that feel as if you're listening to an old friend exposing something of himself, risking something real.

Musically, *Come* is yet another of Prince's delicious blend-
ings of the past four decades of American black pop music. On
the streets of New York, there is reportedly a Stevie Wonder re-
naissance under way; leave it to Prince to tap into that energy
and pepper *Come* with more than a few Wonder-ful melodies.
What's more, not only has Prince been hanging out with Marvin Gaye's daughter, but obviously with the late, great trouble
man's back catalog: the horny twelve-minute title track/aural
aphrodisiac is a natural heir to "Let's Get It On," "You Sure Love
to Ball," and "I Want You."

Which brings us to the sex thing. People who hate Prince
hate Prince because he loves sex. Prince glorifies it out there
in the open, onstage, on record. He opens *Come* by saying, "If
you're eighteen and over, c'mere. I got something for your
mind." It's a hard-to-resist invitation. Because dead or alive,
Prince—with *Come*, his most powerful record in years—provides pleasure and warmth in a cold, cold world.

Wait a sec. Did I say Prince? Scratch that. And forget all
those other ones—Symbolina, TAFKAP, Victor; I think I just
figured out what to call the guy. His name is Lazarus. And he
is funky. ■

Prince Is Going for "The Gold"

October 13

THE BLACK ALBUM IS BACK. *COME* WENT. *THE GOLD EXPE-
rience* and *The Undertaker* are in the can, waiting for emancipation. Can't tell what's coming out of the purple vault without a program? We offer the following tip sheet.

It looks like a grudging truce is being struck between Prince
and his record company of sixteen years, Warner Bros. Records.
Negotiations between Prince's lawyers and Warner Bros. got

under way this week to finally allow Warners to officially release Prince's oft-bootlegged but never released *The Black Album*. Recorded in 1987, Prince reportedly withdrew *The Black Album* because, depending on which version you believe, its hard grooves, explicit gangsta-style subject matter, and electronically altered vocals—Prince thought it so nasty it would damage his relationship with God; or he was in dispute with Warners over its release schedule.

In any event, Prince scotched the sessions and instead recorded and released the more palatable *Lovesexy*. It is unclear whether Prince has given his approval for the release of the record this time around, but Warner's decision to issue *The Black Album* is especially curious, since the main dispute between the label and the artist is that Warners believes Prince saturates his own market by being so prolific. Warner Bros. declined to comment on the situation.

If all goes according to plan, *The Black Album* should hit record stores on Thanksgiving Day, just thirteen weeks after the release of Prince's current release *Come,* which this week dropped to No. 122 on *Billboard*'s Top 200 album chart and to No. 40 on the R&B chart.

According to Karen Lee, Paisley Park's vice president of media communications and publicity, negotiations are also under way between Prince and Warners for the label to release *The Gold Experience*, a finished collection of new Prince material that was originally set for release on the ♀ NPG/Belmark label. Apparently, Prince is extremely antsy to release the record, for which he has already filmed promotional videos. Warner Bros. is reportedly reluctant to issue *The Gold Experience* anytime soon, since the label is still in the process of marketing *Come.*

Yet another in-the-can Prince album is a blues-funk power trio record titled *The Undertaker,* which was conceived with New Power Generation bassist Sonny Thompson and drummer Michael Bland during Christmas vacation last year and recorded at the same time of the *Come* sessions. Of *The Undertaker,* Prince told *Guitar World* magazine: "It's real garage, you know? But Warners won't release it."

As a result of this logjam of material, Prince and the New Power Generation have postponed their planned world tour, which was originally scheduled to open in Australia or Japan this winter. According to Lee, Prince decided to push the tour back until early '95, so audiences will be familiar with the material off *The Gold Experience.*

Last Saturday night, Prince and the NPG performed "Endorphinmachine" on the VH1–Honors show. Each of the eight artists honored chose a charity to which his or her share of the proceeds of ticket sales and ad revenue would go; Prince chose the Westside Preparatory School, an inner city Chicago school. ■

Blast from the Past

Seven Years after Its Recording—and Much to the Chagrin of Prince—Warner Bros. Issues His Much Mythologized *The Black Album*

November 22

TODAY'S OFFICIAL RELEASE OF PRINCE'S *THE BLACK ALBUM* ends the story of one of the most controversial albums in pop music history and begins another chapter in the ongoing—and increasingly volatile—relationship between Prince and his label of sixteen years, Warner Bros. Records.

Recorded in 1987, *The Black Album* was never released because Prince felt its tone was too dark. He pulled it from distribution at the last minute, but not before Warner Bros. had manufactured copies. Since its cancellation, the ten-song work has become one of the most widely bootlegged albums ever, rivaled only by another boot-turned-official release, Bob Dylan and the Band's 1975 *The Basement Tapes*. According to *Musician* magazine, more than 250,000 copies of *The Black Album* have been sold in CD and vinyl form, which doesn't include cassette duplications that have moved through the underground bootleg pipeline. Some copies have fetched as much as $1,000. The official version of the disc will be available today only and will feature all ten original tracks and the original artwork.

But the timing of the release is curious, since Warners and Prince currently are arguing over the release of his new album, *The Gold Experience*, which has been debut-ready for several months. So what's going on? "We are accommodating the artist's wishes," says Warners publicist Bob Merlis.

And why release it now? Merlis says, "He signed an agreement to let us do it. We've wanted to put it out for years. We pressed the album in 1987 and destroyed vast quantities of it. If we didn't want to put it out, why did we make so many? The artist decided he would rather not have it on the market at that time." That's still the case, according to Karen Lee, Prince's spokeswoman:

> He's thoroughly pissed off about it. He had to sign an agreement—I can't go into why—but contractually, he didn't have a choice. He feels like he wrote that album when he was a different person. He was angry, and it wasn't music he ever wanted to get out. How can you tell him, as an artist, what to do with his music? He's like, "I'm in a whole different space now, the world is in a different space; the contribution I want to make doesn't sound like that." And here we are back in the record-company politics again, and he doesn't have a choice.

The odd thing is, relatively dark though the tone of *The Black Album* may be, Prince was a happy camper when he recorded it in the fall of 1987. "Paisley Park was freshly open, and much of the bulk of *The Black Album* was among his first work done there," says Alan Leeds, the former Paisley Park vice president who was Prince's tour manager at the time. Leeds continues:

> Actually, *The Black Album* began with some tracks that he cut specifically as party music for a birthday party that he was throwing for Sheila E. Some of that album was designed as party music, which may or may not mean that he had ideas of ever releasing it. So there was nothing really dark going on in his life; the album started out as very innocuous dance music for a girlfriend, and his dream building, his facility and his company, was growing by leaps and bounds.

Leeds says that part of the impetus of the album was in reaction to hip-hop and to criticism that Prince had sold out the so-called black elements of his music. After pulling *The Black Album*, Prince opted to record *Lovesexy*, a much more sanguine pop record. "It was inspired directly by this epiphany that he went through that dictated to him to cancel *Black Album* and do something that he felt was more uplifting and responsible," says Leeds. As Leeds continues:

> He had some kind of a spiritual awakening that dictated it. Some voice told him, "Don't release that record." The only thing he ever said to me was that if something happened to him, that would be the last statement he made to the public, and he didn't want that to be how he was remembered. So to everybody's chagrin who worked at Warner Bros. and had the thing on the loading dock, it was stopped. Now the true story is that he did make the decision; Warners had nothing to do with stopping the record. It was his sole decision to stop it, and copies were literally on the loading dock, pulled back, and destroyed.

From what Lee says, that's exactly what Prince would like to see done this time around. In fact, he may have foreseen this day coming, for various liner notes and tour programs since

1987 have contained the message, "Don't buy the black album." Told that Prince is upset about the release of the record, Merlis said, "All I can tell you is that October 25, he signed an agreement letting us put it out." Some Prince watchers have speculated that the release of *The Black Album* will go toward fulfilling his Warner Bros. contract, which he has been trying to get out of. Lee, Merlis, or Leeds could not confirm that. Prince declined to be interviewed. "Before they agreed to release *The Black Album*, he owed four albums, and he still owes four albums," says Lee.

Politics aside, *The Black Album* is a worthwhile musical artifact for any Prince fan: "Le Grind" and "Cindy C." (a paean to then-fledgling model Cindy Crawford) are bubbly dance workouts; "When 2 R in Love" is a romantic ballad that finally surfaced on *Lovesexy*; and "Old Friends for Sale" (not included in the official Warner Bros. version) is a brooding ballad that explores the ramifications of the glamorous life. Today, the harder bits of *The Black Album* may sound dated, but the disc as a whole is nonetheless illuminating, a frozen moment that bridges the gap between the fading new-wave pop of the day and the burgeoning gangsta rap of the future.

"It will be really interesting to see if the climate is receptive to it," Leeds says. He goes on:

> I've got a feeling that they're three years late on this. So I don't know what they're gonna accomplish, other than everybody'll make a little cash. Not that that's bad. It's good music, and it deserves to be out there. I was very disappointed, actually, when it was canceled, because I thought it was a fun album. I don't think it's as profound as legend has it. In the long run, I don't think when somebody judges his career twenty years from now, they're going to say that that was an absolute high point. But it's a cool record. Legend made it more important than it is. ■

Prince's Label President and Publicist Resign; Organization Stays Mum on Motives behind Moves

November 30

IN A MAJOR SHAKE-UP AT PRINCE'S PAISLEY PARK STUDIOS, Levi Seacer Jr., the artist's longtime business and music collaborator and president of Prince's Chanhassen-based NPG Records, has resigned. Prince's publicist for the past two years, Karen Lee, also resigned, effective Thursday. Seacer was unavailable for comment, but Lee, reached at home Tuesday where she was packing to move to Los Angeles, said only, "It's time for a change, time to move on." Prince's Los Angeles–based publicist Mitch Schneider of Levine–Schneider Public Relations said, "They left of their own accord, and beyond that there's no other information to report."

There was no word on possible successors.

The resignations come after Prince's Thanksgiving Day performance at the MTV European Music Awards in Berlin. *USA Today* reported Monday that Prince, who changed his name to a symbol on his birthday last year, ordered his spokeswoman to wipe the name "Prince" off any existing promotional posters for the awards program.

The resignations will not affect Prince projects planned for December, including a new release by the New Power Generation called "Get Wild," written and sung by Prince's bassist, Sonny Thompson. The purple entrepreneur uncorks what one source describes as a "poly-gender fragrance" dubbed "Get Wild," which will hit boutique shelves in the spring of 1995. ∎

1995

Prince, Minnesota Politicos Make for Creative Yet Self-Conscious Set

January 17

"I WANT TO THANK EVERYBODY WHO HELPED ORGANIZE this superbad event," Minneapolis Mayor Sharon Sayles Belton said to the six hundred supporters who paid $100 to attend a mayoral fund-raiser at Paisley Park Studios Saturday night. "We're here tonight to enjoy a rehearsal by the greatest musician in the world, a man who put Minnesota on the map." Then, in what was perhaps one of the oddest snapshots in the history of state politics-slash-entertainment, the mayor held up a gold cardboard symbol—the same prop David Letterman used to refer to Prince on the December 13, 1994, segment of the *Late Show with David Letterman*—to introduce the evening's entertainment. After an opening belly dance from dancer/singer Mayte, Prince and the rest of the New Power Generation (bassist Sonny Thompson, drummer Michael Bland, keyboardists Tommy Barbarella and Morris Hayes) took the stage to the strains of "Seven" and launched into an entertaining but musically pretty uninspiring eleven-song, sixty-five-minute performance.

"1994 was a strange one," admitted Prince, who seemed to be in especially good spirits, at one point. "Are we glad it's gone? Yeah. There was one nice thing that happened last year. I made one friend. She goes by the name of Sharon Sayles Belton."

Clad in matching silver-gold lamé pants and vest, and sporting his now-trademark "Slave" etched on the side of his cheek, Prince's relatively safe set list may have been influenced by the bizarre audience mix: well-heeled politicos and society couples in tuxedos and evening gowns mingled with models, teenage Prince diehards and their well-connected parents, and fans who traveled from seven states for the show. That mixture of Minnesota stoicism and NPG fanaticism (and the fact that the dance floor was clogged by rows of folding chairs) made for a formality that is foreign to most Prince gigs.

The lowlights of the night were "Shhh," an otherwise brilliant power ballad that was marred by feedback; a wooden new number called "Get Funky" that generated little energy; and a tepid cover of "Proud Mary" (!). Highlights included a beautiful reading of Martika's anthem, "Love, Thy Will Be Done"; an effervescent version of the bigotry-bashing rave-up "Race"; a refreshingly nasty take on the blues workout "The Ride"; and a sultry new ballad.

The strongest musical moment of the night was a loose, lively version of "Days of Wild," during which Prince, perhaps with the mayor's new low-income housing program in mind, emphasized the lyrics about social decay ("Pop guns and weed, brother, please"), and good-naturedly scolded Hayes, who had put on a rainbow wig. "Highest regard to the honorable mayor," said Prince, as the band cast out a smoldering, organ-driven funk groove. "Much props and much peace in '95. Morris, you're in the mayor's house tonight: you better take that hair off."

During the main set's conclusion, an extended version of "Superhero" for which Prince donned a fedora and electronic keyboard–guitar, he said, "You're all welcome to come to Paisley Park anytime. That's what '95's about." ∎

Evening Was Uneven at Paisley Park

August 7

IN RESPONSE TO A CRITIC'S ASSESSMENT OF A VISUAL ART work as being "uneven," a letter writer to the *New York Times* some years ago argued that the analysis was bogus, because all true art is uneven. She was correct, too, because I can't think of anything less compelling than an "even" work of art. In public-image terms, the Artist Formerly Known as Prince is as uneven as they come these days. And while the gossip-column fodder is too extensive to detail here, over the years he has maintained one constant: the music.

But considering the concert TAFKAP performed at Paisley Park Studios in Chanhassen Saturday night, that's even up for debate. Prince may have scored the sound track to *Batman* in 1989, but the cat who primped and pounded his way through a frisky, funky sixty-minute set was the Riddler all the way. Over eleven songs, the contradictions flew fast and furious for the artist who killed off Prince with the *Come* album last year in order to give TAFKAP room to groove. Clad in a black and white suit peppered with symbols, "Slave" penciled on his right check, and ♀ shaved into his hair above his right ear, he performed several ♀ songs to the five hundred faithful in the house, as well as a few Prince-penned and -recorded songs.

The show opened with a taped version of "I Hate U," from ♀'s forthcoming album *The Gold Experience*. From there, the well-drilled New Power Generation (TAFKAP, singer/dancer Mayte, bassist Sonny Thompson, drummer Michael Bland, keyboardists Morris Hayes and Tommy Barbarella) delivered thirty minutes that felt like a tune-up for a rumored American fall tour. But the second half was an all-out off-the-cuff jam that found the Riddler dipping into Prince's back catalog ("Pink Cashmere," "Letitgo") and firing up a strobe light—

drenched version of "Now," which evolved into a lengthy guitar solo in which ♀ effortlessly married rockabilly and funk licks.

♀ was all business, though also campy and mischievous. At one point, he broke into a version of TLC's "Waterfalls." And near the end, he paid homage to his musical influences by testifying, "You've been entertained by Sgt. Pepper's Lonely Hearts Club Band, Little Richard, the Ohio Players, Jimi Hendrix," and others. But he forgot at least one. In the early '80s, Prince told a journalist that his dream for his band was to be "the black Rolling Stones." But considering this most recent showcase of raw guitar fireworks, a wildly inconsistent (okay, "uneven") set list, and a propensity for melding his past with his future that keeps even his most ardent fans guessing, it might be time to start calling him the artist currently known as the black Neil Young. ∎

People

Geography Lesson

"THIS AIN'T CLEVELAND!" THE ARTIST FORMERLY KNOWN as Prince told a crowd of several hundred Saturday night at Paisley Park Studios in Chanhassen. While the Concert for the Rock and Roll Hall of Fame was going on in Ohio, the former Prince was turning out his own tribute that included covers of the Rolling Stones' "Honky Tonk Women," Elvis Presley's "Jailhouse Rock," Sly & the Family Stone's "Babies Makin' Babies," and James Brown's "Sex Machine."

Early advertisements had ♀ on the bill in Cleveland, but Paisley Park officials insist a deal was never finalized for him to appear at the concert, for which all artists donated their time and performances in a benefit for the Hall of Fame. "He was approached, but he decided not to do it," said a Paisley Park representative. "He does not feel a part of them. He does not feel a part of the system. And for them to suggest in any way that he had committed and then pulled out is unfair, because there was never a contract, and he never, ever, committed to it." ∎

From Chanhassen: As the ♀ Turns

September 22

A♀ CONCERT IS HARDLY STOP-THE-PRESSES MATERIAL anymore—the former Prince and the New Power Generation have performed at Paisley Park's Love 4 One Another dance club close to a dozen times in the past two months. But Tuesday night's jam was newsworthy for a few reasons. First, a cameo appearance was made by keyboardist/superproducer Dallas Austin, the songwriter responsible for several of the '90s biggest hits, including, as ♀ pointed out to the crowd of about three hundred, TLC's "Creep" and Madonna's "Secret." Austin's presence at Paisley lends credence to the rumors that TLC's next single will be a duet with the former Prince on his "If I Was Your Girlfriend," which TLC covered on their last album.

Second, one week before Warner Bros. Records is scheduled to release his new album *The Gold Experience*, ♀ spoke candidly from the stage about his ongoing feud with the record giant, saying, "The latest is that they won't release *The Exodus* [an NPG album that has been distributed overseas] for six months. By that time, it'll be out of style. They have no compassion. They say, 'You signed a piece of paper.' I say, 'Am I a piece of paper?'"

He said it more casually than angrily; despite the flu bug he was fighting, the former Prince seemed to be in good spirits and even joked that the Atlanta-based Austin will produce his next album: "It'll be called 'The Man's Impatient.' It'll be fifty-two songs; eighty dollars. Then all I gotta do is sell a million of 'em, and I can quit. Naw, I ain't gonna quit." ■

Liner Notes for *The Gold Experience*

Released September 26

EARLY ONE MORNING IN FEBRUARY 1993, I WALKED OUT of Minneapolis Glam Slam, where Prince, as he was then known, and the New Power Generation had performed an impromptu concert. It was a three-set marathon, a greatest hits revue that included a version of "Purple Rain" that had the patrons on the floor waving their arms back and forth religiously. Just like in the movie. Just like in the past. When it was over, I made my way across Fifth Street, and as the Minnesota air freeze-dried the dance sweat on my face, I turned up my collar to an entirely different kind of coldness: after establishing himself as one of the most fiercely innovative musical forces in American culture over the past decade, Prince, it seemed, had little left to offer but star power, showmanship, and fuzzy nostalgia.

And the truth is, since I'd seen it happen before, I can't say I was all that disappointed. Instead, I took comfort in the fact that I'd borne witness to the little rocket's ascent more than a dozen times in clubs: at First Avenue (then Sam's) in 1980 the night before he and the *Dirty Mind* band went to Los Angeles to open for the Rolling Stones; in 1981 at an amazing free-form jam the night after the *Controversy* tour stopped at Met Center;

in 1983 at the Minnesota Dance Theater performance at First Avenue where much of *Purple Rain* was recorded; in 1984 the week *Purple Rain* was released; in 1987 at a warm-up for the *Sign o' the Times* tour; at Glam Slam in 1990 working out material for *Graffiti Bridge*; and on and on and on.

But as I walked from the club to the parking ramp that night, I admit to feeling a certain smug sympathy for the nouveau Prince fans who'd just got done paying their respects in the court of His Royal Badness. Because more than anything, the Glam Slam gig reminded me of the times I'd seen Ray Charles and James Brown—in dinner theaters. Entertaining shows, to be sure, but like all such experiences, the music was framed by the specter of pale imitation and a little voice that nagged, "You should've been there when . . ."

Overnight, then, it seemed as if Prince had prematurely signed on with this relic club, trading spontaneity for choreography, risks for hits, genius for just good enough—all of which is and always has been anathema to his legendary appetite for self-experimentation. At the time, the word on the street was that Prince was old news, that he'd been displaced by an army of new jacks who couldn't run with him on a real instrument if their entire collection of vinyl samples depended on it.

Which is why, when the strains of "Purple Rain" finally faded that night and I watched Prince take his bows, I wondered if he suspected what I did. I wondered if he realized that the stuff was just this side of stale, and if he had it in him to challenge himself again. Nobody could blame him if he wanted to coast after all these years, but as I watched him run through an admittedly mind-blowing array of old hits, another, very distinct, impression took hold: that he was bored out of his skull, and he was purging himself of his past.

Fast-forward exactly one year later. Prince is no longer Prince but a symbol/glyph, and everyone, including me, thinks he's gone off the deep end. Later, he'll tell Alan Light from *Vibe* magazine that he knows people will make jokes about it—he even accepts that aspect of it—but that the name change is a way to draw a very clear line between him and the comfort of his past laurels. Weirdly, I get it. On a gut level, I understand his desire for his music to grow, his need to move on, and his thirst for personal growth. Maybe it's because he and I are the same age and grew up in virtually the same neighborhood, but in my thirty-sixth year I likewise discovered that true knowledge doesn't come easy; it requires a process that psychotherapists call "hard work" and that Prince calls panning for "gold."

Which is to say that Prince doesn't represent the past, but possibility. In February 1994, he emerged from an intense writing and recording seclusion and threw a party (The Beautiful Experience) at Paisley Park to commemorate the release of "The Most Beautiful Girl in the World" single. That's when I first heard much of the material you now hold in your hands—including the marvelous cartoon dance workout "Now" and the Al Green–kissed "Most Beautiful Girl." The ninety-minute performance was a gritty, lean, and supremely nasty coming-out baptism that, unlike the Glam Slam gig a mere twelve months prior, revealed Prince to be a past-jettisoning, forward-thinking world citizen capable of howling lines like "Hooker, bitch, 'ho, I don't think so," and then, with genuine bad-ass squirreliness, "Light us up and take a hit."

Which, as a matter of fact, is exactly what I did. As often as possible. Last summer, Prince and the NPG set up shop for a week in Erotic City, the small annex in Minneapolis Glam Slam's upper deck. Typically, they'd start at about 2:00 A.M. and play until 3:00. All my cronies from the old days had long since given in to their skepticism and bailed from the purple magic bus, so my friend Theresa Sheehy was the only one I could ever talk into going. One night we were joined by 150 people. The next, four hundred. One night, he lay on his back and played feathery blues guitar for twenty minutes; the next, he bounced off the NPG horns like a tireless, tenacious Muscle

Shoals band leader; the next, he led three hundred people on a scavenger hunt out to Chanhassen for a full-fledged concert at Paisley Park.

It was exhilarating, and exhausting. Theresa and I would drive home from those gigs dazed and bemused, and go to sleep with the birds chirping and the sun coming up. The next day, we'd call each other up: Did you hear this? What was that lyric? What's up with the spiritual vibe? I was floored by the band—bassist Sonny T., drummer Michael Bland, keyboardists Tommy Barbarella and Mr. Hayes—and the balance they struck between well-drilled professionalism and off-the-cuff jam-ability. After a July Glam Slam gig, Theresa said she thought "Pussy Control" was just another one of Prince's sexist throwaways; I thought that was too easy. I defended it as a lighthearted and raunchy take on the power of womanhood.

We bitched, wondered, and danced. Yeah, we were hooked, I suppose in the same way that any Prince fan gets hooked, but because it was all new material and we were hearing it as works in progress unfettered by the usual cheese, it was more exciting than just superstar-gazing in a small club. It was, as we often said those nights in June and July, like discovering an underground band that nobody had ever heard of before.

In retrospect, it was exactly what I needed. I'd spent much of the last year of my job at the *St. Paul Pioneer Press* covering the music of despair, and I was sick of everybody being so damned serious. I wanted to have some fun. Prince and the NPG did it; they made me laugh and think and twitch. And there was something else: after spending the past few years cultivating personas of soft-rock balladeer, electrifying dancer, and public relations goofball, Prince returned to doing what he does better than almost anyone else on the planet: *playing guitar*. Upon first hearing Jimi Hendrix's "Purple Haze," Bruce Gary wrote that "it was as if all the soul music and rock 'n' roll I'd ever heard had become this raging flood." That quote stuck in my head night after night as Prince consistently nailed my jaw to the floor and swept us all up in his own raging, gushing flash flood.

As the summer wore on, Prince started showing up for more impromptu gigs at Glam Slams in Miami and Los Angeles, and the grapevine reported that he was performing this brilliant new material side by side with covers by Stevie Wonder, Sly Stone, and Salt-N-Pepa. He's never made a secret of his passion for musical history, and you can clearly hear the bridging of those three generations folded into these grooves. It's there in the anthemic utopian vision-meets-celebrity vulnerability of "Gold," in the hard-won, socially conscious confidence of "We March," and in the jubilant noise that is "Now." Pissed off and playful all at once, it also contains a genuine bitterness and anger at the media that cuts through on "Billy Jack Bitch." As that track illustrates, *The Gold Experience* is, if nothing else, raw and real. And in case you haven't been paying attention, that's big news. One of my main complaints about so much modern R&B is that everything sounds so unremittingly chipper; even supposedly sad torch songs are rendered with a glossy detachment, an anti-feeling. No such problem here: "Shhh" is a melancholy blues-gospel jam built on a tangible bed of longing, while "I Hate U" is a messy, anguish-filled kiss-off that stems from a paradox (desire versus spite) that more polite art usually avoids.

Above all, Prince wants it known that this is a record about the fight for freedom—personal, artistic, political—but anyone with half an ear can suss that much out. During the making of it, he was enamored with Betty Eadie's book *Embraced by the Light,* a first-person narrative on near-death experience, and that theme also peppers the record, most explicitly on the reincarnation dream "Dolphin." It is also implicit on several other tracks that ponder birth, death, life, and rebirth, and one man's own expectations and perceptions of himself.

To me, the most fascinating aspect about these twelve songs is that they come from a human being who, like you and me, struggles day in and day out, but unlike you and me, does so in a very public forum. And that public flailing makes the music somehow resonate even deeper and transcend the confines of good beats and hit making. It is the sound of an artist at odds with himself, his world, his past, present, and future. Who would've guessed that such a sound could be this big, bad, and joyful?

More than anything, throughout my own *Gold* experience, I heard a unique, and uniquely potent, mix of purpose, celebration, and fear. There is a palpable sense of urgency here, as if Prince knows that time is running out for all of us to make connections with ourselves and the outside world. Don't believe me? Listen to the scream in the middle of "Endorphinmachine" or the guitar solo on "Gold" that concludes the album. The two things they share are desperation and liberation. Listen. Cue 'em up, back to back. Hear it? He isn't showing off; he's searching. Again. And like never before.

Hold on to your wig. ∎

Prince Pullout from *SNL* Tests Patience of Faithful

September 28

IT SEEMED LIKE A GOOD IDEA AT THE TIME: A MERE FIVE days after the release of his long-delayed album *The Gold Experience*, the Artist Formerly Known as Prince would get a much-needed image boost, not to mention valuable publicity for his new record, by appearing as the musical guest on the season premiere of *Saturday Night Live*, which airs Saturday. The Chanhassen-based musician agreed to the terms of the appearance and even confirmed as much during a recent performance at Paisley Park's short-lived dance club, claiming that he and his band, the New Power Generation, were going to "tear s___ up" on the show. And even as late as last Saturday night, NBC was running promos publicizing the former Prince's appearance, along with guest host Mariel Hemingway.

But Monday morning, Paisley Park informed NBC that the former Prince had changed his mind and pulled out. He has since been replaced by Blues Traveler. A source at Paisley suggested that the cancellation stems from the musician's ongoing feud with his label, Warner Bros. Records, and that he isn't spiritually, physically, or emotionally ready to perform.

The *Saturday Night Live* cancellation is only the latest episode to test the patience of the former Prince's loyal fan base, who have been ridiculed for defending the artist's antics, be it his name-to-symbol change, his etching of the word "slave" on his face, or an ongoing music-industry war story that has all but eclipsed his music.

"That sucks," said longtime Prince fan Bridget Richardson, when told of the *SNL* reversal. "But at the same time, I just don't blame him, dealing with all this Warner Bros. crap. But he's losing so many people, especially in the mainstream, who just go, 'Oh, brother. Here he goes again.' I think people are done trying to figure out [the Warner Bros. feud]. They think he's a freak."

Still, Richardson isn't about to give up on the music. "I just love him too much," she said. "It's like a weird relationship. I'm mad, but I don't blame him. It's like the song 'I Hate U': 'I hate you because I love you.'"

According to Daniel Ferguson, senior press manager for NBC-TV late night programming, there are no plans for a makeup date. ■

People

Rock 'n' Roles

F IVE HUNDRED FUNK FANS GATHERED AT PAISLEY PARK Studios Saturday night/Sunday morning to participate in a video shoot by ♀ and the New Power Generation. Three songs were captured on the reels: "Days of Wild," "Gold," and "Rock 'n' Roll Is Alive (and It Lives in Minneapolis!)," the latter slated to be released as the B-side of the next single from ♀'s *The Gold Experience*, which debuted at No. 6 on the *Billboard* pop charts last week. All patrons entering the Paisley premises were asked to sign a petition urging Warner Bros. Records to release the NPG album *The Exodus*.

During a short post–video-shoot performance, which ended with an unexpected version of "Starfish and Coffee" from the 1987 *Sign o' the Times* album, ♀ thanked "the beloved Time Warner for releasing *The Gold Experience*" and dedicated "Love, Thy Will Be Done" to the media giant.

"Rock 'n' Roll Is Alive" was written in response to Lenny Kravitz's "Rock 'n' Roll Is Dead" and contains what could be interpreted as a dig at Elvis "The King" Presley and/or Michael "The King of Pop" Jackson: "Sure as the drive around Lake of the Isles is cool, I know rock 'n' roll will never die, like the Minnehaha flow, sure as the land of 10,000 lakes is sometimes made of snow, there will always be another king to die butt-naked on the floor." ∎

Former Prince Presents Fans with Early Christmas Gift

December 12

F IVE HUNDRED FANS OF THE ARTIST FORMERLY KNOWN AS Prince received an early Christmas present Saturday night in the form of a two-hour concert at Paisley Park Studios in Chanhassen. The show, which included several old Prince songs and a recorded cover version of Joan Osborne's "One of Us," was a dress rehearsal for the former Prince and the New Power Generation's tour that kicks off in Japan next month. The concert, which started at 11:30 P.M., also acted as the latest episode in the former Prince's ongoing war with Warner Bros., his record company of seventeen years. As fans entered the building, they were presented with a new TAFKAP cassette single, "Slave." The chorus asserts: "I just want the chance to play the part, the part of someone truly free."

Over the years, Prince has been one of pop music's most prolific musicians and has always had side projects into which he funneled excess material. But when his own label, Paisley Park Records, went belly-up earlier this year, the former Prince was left with virtually himself—and solo records by NPG singer-dancer Mayte and the New Power Generation—as his only vehicles for self-expression. That creative bridle, along with an apparent suspicion of the new administration at Warner Bros. Records, has reportedly been TAFKAP's main grievance with the company. "My name is 'Slave' until I get free," he told the crowd, then implored them to chant, "Prince is dead." Later, he declared that the name of the tour would be Emancipation, the same title of an album he reportedly plans to uncork upon his release from his Warner Bros. contract.

"Whatchou all think?" ♀ asked the crowd near the end of the show. "Think we got a shot on the big circuit? I know a few people who think otherwise. They wear suits and ties and they live in L.A."

But beyond the distracting name and business squabbles that filled the between-song patter, the sixteen-song concert suggested that Japan and whatever other countries are on the tour itinerary (no U.S. dates have been announced) are in for a treat. The set offered recent TAFKAP material, including "Days of Wild," "We March," "I Hate U," and "The Most Beautiful Girl in the World." Midway through, TAFKAP coyly said, "We'd like to do a couple of cover tunes by one of my favorite artists. Goes by the name o' Prince." From there, the band went into "Letitgo," "Starfish and Coffee," "The Cross," "Do Me, Baby," "Sexy M.F.," "If I Was Your Girlfriend," and "Seven."

At the end of an especially impassioned "Love, Thy Will Be Done," the former Prince stepped to the microphone and said: "This is all we want to do. We don't want to have no problem with nobody. There's enough music to go around."

The set ended with a metallic recorded cover of Osborne's beautiful alterna-folk hit "One of Us." In keeping with the night's theme of freedom, he changed the lyric from "What if God was one of us, just a slob like one of us?" to "What if God was one of us, just a slave like one of us?"

———

Immediately after this set, Prince's Paisley publicist Julie Winge came up to me at my spot by the soundboard and said, "The boss wants to see you." I said good-bye to some friends, and then Winge took me upstairs to Prince's office, which consisted of a couple of couches, a stereo system, speakers, a fax machine, a computer, and a desk.

I sat down on the couch; he stood behind his desk. The meeting lasted less than five minutes. "I'm going to Japan," he said, "and I just wanted you to know that I have reason to be concerned, and if anything happens to me . . . I just wanted you to know. That's all."

"That's it?" I said.

*He was done talking. I said, "Okay, just to be clear: are you telling
me you think someone, or the music industry, is going to rub you out
while you're on tour?"*

*He raised one eyebrow and cocked his head into a question mark.
I told him if anything happened to him, I would report our conversation to the world and look into it, and it's the first thing I thought of
the day after he died, when Dick Gregory and other conspiracy theo-
rists claimed that Prince didn't die from an accidental drug overdose,
but that "they" had murdered him.* ■

Free at Last?

December 23

ACCORDING TO A PRESS RELEASE ISSUED BY PAISLEY PARK
Enterprises Friday, the Artist Formerly Known as Prince
has officially notified his label, Warner Bros. Records, of his desire to terminate his recording agreement with the company.
The release states:

> Over the course of their nearly two decade long relationship,
> the artist and WBR have developed irreconcilable differences.
> Most recently, the unstable and ever changing management
> structure within WBR has made it impossible for the com-
> pany to effectively market and promote its flagship artists, in-
> cluding ♀.
>
> The Artist is prepared to deliver three (3) remaining al-
> bums under his former name Prince, which will fulfill his con-
> tractual obligation to WBR. Currently, the albums are titled:
> *Prince: The Vault—Volumes I, II, and III.*
>
> ♀ will release a new recording entitled *Emancipation* once
> he is free from all ties with Time Warner.

A spokesperson for Warner Bros. was unavailable for comment. ■

1996

Prince's Uptown Store Closes

SINCE IT OPENED ON AUGUST 4, 1993, THE DISPLAY WINDOW at the New Power Generation store at 1408 West Lake Street in Minneapolis has displayed dozens of Prince-related items—posters, gold and platinum records, perfume, satin drapes, and the chain-link mask the singer wore in the "My Name Is Prince" video. But one week into 1996, a sign went up: "Closed for remodeling." Then last week, the mementos were taken out of the window, and two new hastily scribbled signs o' the times popped up: "Closed" and "For merchandise call 474-1751 or 1-800-New-Funk."

For the past few years, the former Prince has sold much of his wares by mail order, but as of Monday, the 800 number had been disconnected. The new number is an extension at Paisley Park Studios in Chanhassen. On Monday, a worker reached at the number maintained the store's closing was not permanent but truly closed for remodeling: "They're rewiring something in there. Or something."

At the Mall of America, a New Power Generation cart was a fixture for the past two years, but according to a mall representative, "The cart hasn't been around for six months or so." During its tenure, the New Power Generation store has become the preferred one-stop for fans of the former Prince. Hard-to-find albums, videos, T-shirts, guitar picks, condoms ("Purple Raincoat," natch), and other trinkets could be purchased there. It also featured a video viewing room and housed the convertible used in Prince's 1988 *Lovesexy* tour.

But like that ride, it would appear the NPG store is another relic from long-gone glory days and further testament to what looks to be the former Prince's continuing spiral downward in the commercial marketplace. Although his latest album, *The Gold Experience,* recently was certified gold (500,000 copies sold), sources say the artist's tour of Japan earlier this month played to half-filled halls.

The closing of the New Power Generation store comes on the heels of the recent news of the sale of the former Prince's Los Angeles mansion and the closings of, or his disassociation with, Glam Slam clubs in Minneapolis, Miami, and Los Angeles. ■

Mayte Aphrodite

So, What's the Story behind This Woman Who Managed to Get the Former Prince to Say "I Do"? Well, She's . . .

February 14

"ALL OF MY PURPLE LIFE, I'VE BEEN LOOKING FOR A DATE that would want to be my wife . . ," sang Prince on the opening of "Erotic City," the B-side to his 1984 single "Let's Go Crazy." Well, what a difference twelve years makes. Prince is no longer Prince but ♀, and if the gossip columnists, fan club members, and publicists are to be believed, the purple one has found his soulmate.

That would be Mayte Garcia, a twenty-four-year-old native of Puerto Rico who is rumored to be wedding the former Prince today in Paris.

How did they meet? Local legend has it that Mayte was so intrigued by "Thieves in the Temple," a song from Prince's 1990 album *Graffiti Bridge,* that she made contact with Prince. A classically trained dancer, Mayte sent Prince videos of her dance career, one of which was from the old television talent show *That's Incredible!* The clip is included on *Three Chains o' Gold,* a home video compilation that's basically a showcase for Mayte, and easily the cheesiest project that has ever been coughed up by Paisley Park. But for pure camp factor, its saving grace is the clip of *That's Incredible!* host John Davidson, who introduces "the mystical, magical, eight-year-old Princess Mayte." Onscreen comes the preadolescent Mayte, who dances an Arabic routine in which she balances a sword on her head, does a belly dance, and rolls quarters on her stomach, a trick she reprised on the *Arsenio Hall Show* in 1993. According to *Uptown*, the official Prince fan club magazine, Mayte spent her youth traveling the world with her military father and her mother, a language teacher, and spent a considerable amount of time in Cairo, Egypt, the setting for *Three Chains o' Gold*.

Since then, Mayte has become an official member of the former Prince's band, the New Power Generation. Her main duty has been as erotic visual foil for the Minneapolis superstar and as cheerleader/tambourine player who helps ignite the crowd. She also is a singer. Her debut album, released by NPG Records/Edel in November, is called *Child of the Sun*, and her single, "If I Love U 2 Night" (which originally appeared on the 1994 compilation *1-800-New-Funk*), has produced an artsy steamy video that debuted on VH1 January 27.

Rumors flew at the end of last year that the former Prince and Mayte had already secretly wed. In November and December, Mayte took to wearing flowing white gowns in concert and rocking a baby doll in her arms at the lip of the stage. Near the end of a January 17 concert in Tokyo, the former Prince said, "I don't know when we'll come around here again, but I know one thing: when we do, I'll be a married man."

Anyone questioning the validity of the marriage need only to have seen the duo during the Time's set at First Avenue last week. At one point, during "Gigolos Get Lonely, Too," Time lead singer Morris Day cracked, "Sometimes when I'm up here, even though I'm surrounded by these great musicians and a great audience like you, I get really lonely. Can you relate? Is there anyone out there who knows what I'm talking about?" At that, the former Prince—who up until then had sat placidly in First Avenue's second-level deejay booth for most of the show with Mayte—jumped up from his chair, raised his hand in solidarity, clapped, and whistled. Then he caught himself, sat down, and resumed snuggling with his bride-to-be.

Fifteen Symbols of Love

IN HONOR OF VALENTINE'S DAY (and the royal nuptials), here's one man's list of the former Prince's top fifteen love songs:

"Nothing Compares 2 U." An instant classic that the ever-prolific Prince gave to Sinead O'Connor, whose no-holds-barred vocal took it to another stratosphere. That rarest of songs, which can make lovers pine for each other—even when they're right next to each other.

"Do Me, Baby." Unlike the clumsier "Head" or "Sister" of the same era, this is vintage Prince at his raunchy best. A make-out song for the ages.

"I Would Die 4 U." An echo-drenched, drum machine–swathed testimonial of endless love worthy of Romeo or Juliet.

"A Case of You." Oft-bootlegged cover of the Joni Mitchell gem, performed (to my knowledge) just once, at the July 1983 benefit for the Minnesota Dance Theater at First Avenue. At the time, Prince never performed covers, which made this lithe, liberating performance even more special.

"I Could Never Take the Place of Your Man." Wonderfully ambiguous tune from the left field of *Sign o' the Times*. Such an exquisite slice of perfect pop rock, the Replacements saw fit to cover it.

"Dirty Mind." Carnal knowledge as show tune.

"Pink Cashmere." An invitation to turn the lights down low and slow dance, very closely, with a very close friend.

"How Come U Don't Call Me Anymore?" Backed by a piano,

this bluesy B-side to "1999" features one of the finest vocal performances of his career. A toss-off, perhaps, but every time I hear it, I dream of the day when he'll make a record with just him, a piano, and his songs.

"I Wanna Be Your Lover." This is the one that made the world sit up and take notice, and for good reason: bubbly rhythm-guitar track, seamless groove, smoking guitar solo, and a coy come-on that goes, "I don't want to pressure you, baby, but all I ever wanted to do . . ."

"If I Was Your Girlfriend." While his social commentary occasionally leaves something to be desired, when the former Prince philosophizes about amour, he can come up with simple twists of genius. Such as: "If I was your girlfriend, would you let me dress you, and help you pick out your clothes before we go out? / Not that you're helpless, but sometimes, that's what being in love is about."

"U Got the Look." Boy versus girl in the World Series of love. One of the little guy's all-time catchiest grooves, this cartoon-funk duet with Sheena Easton is great fun.

"Kiss." If this spare classic doesn't make you wanna dance, then your name is Ricky Rigormortis.

"Raspberry Beret." A tantalizing, effortless rocker that captures that specific kind of initial infatuation that a boy gets about a girl—fixating over not personality or even looks, but over something that catches the eye: a haircut, smile, glance, or yes, a raspberry beret.

"Little Red Corvette." Dark, mysterious, cocksure, and wholly original, with a little *Equus* story line thrown in for good measure.

"The Most Beautiful Girl in the World." Reputedly inspired by Mayte, this lush crooner harkens back to the "women, not girls, rule my world" feminism of "Kiss." ■

Purple Hearts

Prince's Marriage Gives Lift to Inner City
Neighborhood

P ARK AVENUE UNITED METHODIST CHURCH, LOCATED AT
Thirty-fourth Street and Park Avenue in South Minneapolis, is the kind of brick and mortar structure they don't make
anymore. Next to the church is a Sunday school and a small
health clinic. On Wednesday, the marquee in front of the
church advertised the topic for Sunday's sermon—"The Road
to Reconciliation"—and encouraged worshipers to "Celebrate
Black History Month."

Pam Willis and her husband, John, were married in the
church in May 1992. Wednesday, the twenty-four-year-old
Minneapolis native stood across the street from the church
with her ten-month-old son, Alexander, in a backpack, watching the spectacle that her neighborhood had become. "I heard
the helicopters and had to come over," she said. "My husband
has lived in this neighborhood all his life, and the only time
it ever gets any attention is when something negative happens—like a shooting. It's nice to have something positive."
And the Prince–Mayte wedding produced a positive scene—
or at least a positive commotion. Head Start vans and school
buses full of giggling kids jockeyed for space with stretch limousines. The media rubbed elbows with neighborhood folks
and rubberneckers.

This is an area of Minneapolis where the crime rate is high.
But it also is a place where people have roots and history. In
the summer, the place gears up for neighborhood basketball
leagues and the annual Soul Liberation festival, at which gospel groups throw down in the church parking lot.

It also is where Prince Rogers Nelson decided to have his
wedding. So what if nobody got so much as a glimpse of him, or

if Park Avenue was his second choice of location? Prince could have gotten married anywhere—Paris, London, the Basilica of Saint Mary, or the Cathedral of St. Paul—but he chose his old stomping grounds. He picked the place where he learned his craft, played basketball, formed bands, and attended high school at the now-torn-down Minneapolis Central.

Across the street and a few doors down from Park Avenue United Methodist is a house with boarded-up windows and a red condemned sign. On the very same block, there also are some very beautiful homes. "They're all beautiful houses," said Larry Williams. Williams lives directly across the street from the church. He and his wife, Marcelle, have lived there for twenty-seven years and have raised three children and three grandchildren there.

"My middle son went to Central the same year as Prince," the fifty-five-year-old Williams said, craning his neck out the front door to see what the crowd was screaming about Wednesday. "This neighborhood used to be made up of old Swedes and Norwegians. Eric Sevareid's family used to live down the street. Eddie Albert, too."

Williams, a taxi driver, invited me into his kitchen for a cup of coffee to talk about the neighborhood that absorbed so much attention. "The worst thing I've had happen here was in 1973, when some professional stained-glass window thieves came and took the windows," he said. "I just spent $20,000 remodeling the attic. My main thing this morning was I wanted to get the ice off the front sidewalk, so I started chopping at 9 A.M. I don't care what people think of the neighborhood. It's home."

By late afternoon, the intersection at Thirty-fourth and Park was back to normal. The TV crews and gawkers were gone and Larry Williams was able to get back to work on his sidewalk. And Pam and Alexander Willis could take a stroll around the block. At a time when most discussions about the inner city center on urban decay and suburban flight, on Wednesday a millionaire rock star came home to celebrate Valentine's Day in a region of the city that most people avoid like a leper colony. ■

Couple Hadn't Appeared by 11, but Party Guests Heard New Tune

February 15

B Y 11 P.M. WEDNESDAY, THE HAPPY COUPLE HAD NOT showed at an open-to-the-public party at Prince's Paisley Park Studios in Chanhassen. The event was a benefit for the singer's Love for One Another Building Fund. About three hundred guests—family, friends, and fans, no celebrities—paid $25 apiece to get in. Among the highlights from the celebration: the wedding feast included a fabulous-tasting cake (lemony vanilla) and sandwiches, cheeses, and white chocolate dolphin candies. No alcohol was served.

New Power Generation played the song "Friend, Lover, Sister, Mother/Wife," a new Prince composition. The song has been recorded, but no release date is planned.

The foyer at Paisley Park contained a cage with two doves, photographs of Prince and Mayte, a chronicle of how they met, gold spheres hanging from the ceiling, and two giant kissing dolphins.

Bird's-Eye View

SECURITY WAS INCREDIBLY TIGHT at Park Avenue United Methodist Church, but one longtime Prince fan who was not on the guest list nevertheless managed to view the top-secret nuptials. "It was a very Minnesota-like wedding," the observer said, "very emotional and very common."

Or as common as it could be, considering the groom wore a pale peach suit—more like a tuxedo than a tunic—and carried a gold staff. The bride wore a reddish, nontraditional wedding dress and was escorted down the aisle by her father, Major John Garcia. He was in full dress blues. The best man was Prince's good friend Kirk Johnson, who introduced the singer to Mayte. Our source (who requested anonymity because the person who let him inside could get in big trouble) said the couple exchanged rings—Prince's is a gold band with a heart symbol and Mayte's has a big diamond—and embraced as they were pronounced husband and wife.

New Glyph

HE'S CHANGED HIS NAME AGAIN—but it's temporary.

At his open-to-the-public wedding reception Wednesday night at Paisley Park Studios in Chanhassen, the Artist Formerly Known as Prince and ⚥ adopted a new unpronounceable name. The combined ⚥ and *M* was printed in gold ink on paper napkins and is a one-day-only profession of love by TAFKAP for his new spouse. ■

Alone Again Eventually

April 21

THE WALL OF STUDIO B AT PAISLEY PARK STUDIOS IN Chanhassen is adorned with a huge painted mural that immortalizes such quasi-fictional Prince-created locales as Alphabet Street and Graffiti Bridge. One day last October, Paul Westerberg was standing in front of the wall, putting the finishing touches on "Love Untold." It is one tune from his new

album, *Eventually* (in stores April 30), a patchwork collage of
home demos and sessions recorded in Atlanta with producers
Brendan O'Brien and Lou Giordano in Los Angeles and Minneapolis.

Westerberg plugged in his guitar, put on the headphones,
and played an effortless rhythm track. The sight of the former
Replacements leader, sporting blue-tinted prescription eye-
glasses, playing a studied guitar part, and flanked by a Graffiti
Bridge, was a scene fraught with irony to anyone who came up
on the Minneapolis Sound over the past decade. In the '80s,
Westerberg and Prince were instrumental in making up that
so-called sound, and at the time they had little in common.

Now they share a lot. Both have been in disputes with their
record company, Warner Bros. (Westerberg's beef, with Reprise,
has since been resolved), and both have worked with Michael
Bland, Prince's drummer for the past seven years (Bland was
let go, along with the rest of the New Power Generation, on
March 9), who recorded three tracks with Westerberg at Paisley and will tour with him in June. But more than anything,
both no longer are the flavor of the moment—a role Westerberg almost embraces.

On a chilly afternoon last October, Westerberg took time
out from recording what would seven months later be *Eventually* to talk about his art, his life, Prince, and the death of his
friend and former bandmate, Bob Stinson. He sits in a small
waiting room adjacent to Studio B, nursing a can of ginger ale
and puffing a cigarillo.

Q: Prince and the NPG have been down the hall rehearsing
    the whole time you've been here. In the '80s, you two
    pretty much ruled the Minneapolis Sound, or whatever
    you want to call it. Do you see any correlation between
    your career and his?

A: I wonder. I can't honestly say that I do. Other than the
    fact that we're both washed up. No . . . just kidding. I

mean, I talk to Michael [Bland], and they rehearse every day. And I'm like, who could rehearse every day, unless you lived and breathed music like he does? He is a musician, and he would probably die if he didn't have it every day. And for me, that hasn't changed. He's always been a great musician: if he's a pop star or he's in vogue is irrelevant. Like Coltrane or Sly Stone, he's creative, he's great. His new record is always going to be worth a listen to anyone who loves music. What goes on in his brain and what stunts he has to pull to create the publicity to feed his thing, it doesn't affect me. Everyone says, "What's his name?" or "Blah, blah, blah." To me, it's an amusing chuckle. He's the [stuff]. He's a great, great musician. And in a way, I think that I am—you know, not as great—but maybe more of a songwriter. I am a musician and a writer, and I'll always be. And if I'm hip or if I'm an old man, that shouldn't really matter. I'm gonna do this forever, and I think we have that in common.

Q: The song "Good Day" seems to be about Bob [Stinson, the ex-Replacements guitarist who died in February 1995]. How did his death change you?

A: It made me closer to everyone who loved Bob. It just did. In a lot of ways, the "Good Day" song is a song for all of us who are still here, who knew Bob. And a closeness with Tommy [Stinson] and Peter [Jesperson] that was always there, but once again. So if there's any good that ever comes of something like that, it's that. Because it's like, "God, man, one of these days, one of us is gonna go."

Q: We're going to go to a lot more funerals.

A: Yeah. And birthday parties, too. ∎

Ex-Innovator Ex-Prince Serves Leftovers

July 5

TRUMAN CAPOTE ONCE ISSUED ONE OF THE MOST MEM-
orable one-liners in book-reviewing history: "That's not
writing. It's typing."

A similar thing could be said about the Artist Formerly
Known as Prince's new album, *Chaos & Disorder*, which hits
stores Tuesday. Unlike the bulk of the Prince/TAFKAP catalog, *Chaos & Disorder* appears to be an uninspired collection of
warmed-over jams, sketches, snatches, and leftovers.

With apologies to Capote, it's not record making. It's recording. Which, no matter what your feelings are about the
former Prince's public image, has never been the case before.
He may be unfathomable to most anyone outside the music
world, but whenever he gets in the studio, he has always been
consistently innovative, and usually something interesting (at
the least) occurs. Not this time.

Even his previously tossed-off works—the hastily composed *Lovesexy* (1988), the Batphoned-in *Batman* (1989), and
the underrated *Come* (1994)—had unifying themes. But for the
first time, TAFKAP has released an album that sounds void of
his usually visceral focus and inspiration. Beyond the shock
appeal he has become known for, Prince with almost every one
of his seventeen previous albums has always given fans and
critics plenty to chew on musically and lyrically. But on *Chaos
& Disorder*, the disappointing follow-up to last year's *The Gold
Experience*, there is a creeping feeling of déjà vu—a feeling that
even if we haven't heard these particular musings on love, sex,
spirituality, human rights, and the afterlife, we've heard him
do it before. And better.

The Warner Bros. bio for *Chaos & Disorder* would have us believe that this is another guitar record, on a par with the fire-

works that fuel *The Gold Experience*. But where those were lithe, compact, and purposeful moments, the guitar work on *Chaos & Disorder* is typically flashy but emotionally stingy. I admit that I yearn to hear ex-Prince dueling with a second guitar again, in order to bring in da funk, bring in da noise. Perhaps the biggest shame about *Chaos & Disorder* is that it does a disservice to the reputation of the otherwise spectacular New Power Generation—so regal and powerful on *The Gold Experience*—which sounds an awful lot like a band being put through its paces or on the verge of getting the pink slip (which happened earlier this year).

Even TAFKAP's ubiquitous ear candy is applied much too literally to be compelling: revving motors behind a lyric about cars, a radio deejay behind a lyric about Top 40 radio, a moaning woman behind a lyric about orgasm, a siren behind a lyric about domestic abuse, etc.

Once upon a time, the former Prince would throw in a sound bite that gave the track a freaky quality. It made the song blow up in your headphones and imagination. But here, everything is carefully scripted for the listener. As a result, *Chaos & Disorder* is sonically stuck in the '80s, at a moment in time when Beck's *Odelay* and others set the standard for cutting-edge recording artistry.

Maybe the reason *Chaos & Disorder* is so disappointing concerns the high standards TAFKAP sets and usually hits. And, of course, as with any TAFKAP album, there are some choice morsels to go along with the leftovers. By my count, there are four strong cuts:

"Chaos & Disorder." The record kicks off with a bang, thanks to this wicked quasi-antidrug rocker's bloody-raw vocal performance.

"Same December." A hopped-up big band rave on race relations, punctuated by the scintillating NPG horns. Lyrically, it's the latest in a long line of utopian visions from Prince/

TAFKAP. Musically, it features a chorus worthy of T. Rex, a hook worthy of classic Prince, and it could be a monster hit for a radio format that doesn't exist.

"I Rock Therefore I Am." An irresistible dance hall number buoyed by the NPG horns and cameo vocals and reggae raps from Rosie Gaines, Scrap D., and Steppa Ranks.

"Dig U Better Dead." A genuinely weird and thoroughly ebullient dance workout that can stand with the nastiest mechanigrooves in the Prince catalog.

The rest of *Chaos & Disorder* is remarkably unremarkable. (Has there ever been a more forgettable Prince single than "Dinner with Delores"?) Which brings us to the conspiracy theory. *Chaos & Disorder* is the last studio album the former Prince is required to release on Warner Bros. Records, his record company since 1978. (A forthcoming three-CD set of outtakes and unreleased material, *The Vault,* is reportedly the final release, which will fulfill his contract.) Given all that, and the fact that his first album was titled *For You,* the last song on this CD, the one-minute-twenty-six-second "Had U," could be read as a final kiss-off from the Slave to Warner Bros. I do not believe, as some do, that the former Prince has hit his creative ceiling. But the truth is, as he sings on "Zannalee," "If you want a headline, you've gotta be all you can be," and I hope that *Chaos & Disorder* is just the dusk before the dawn. ■

Former Prince Crowned Minnesota's Top Music Artist

July 12

HERE'S A COMPLETE LIST OF THE WINNERS FROM THE 1996 Minnesota Music Awards, which were presented Thursday night at First Avenue:

Artist of the Year: The Artist Formerly Known as Prince

Song of the Year: Paul Westerberg, "Good Day"

Male Songwriter of the Year: Paul Westerberg

Female Songwriter of the Year: Barb Cohen

Major Label Album: Golden Smog, *Down by the Old Mainstream*

Independent Label Album: Eller Lynch, *Dog Day Afternoon*

Self-Produced Album: Barb Cohen & Little Lizard, *Black Lake*

Electric Guitarist of the Year: Billy Franze (Billy Franze Trio)

Acoustic Guitarist of the Year: Billy McLaughlin

Bassist of the Year: Jim Anton (Greazy Meal, Eight Head)

Drummer of the Year: Noah Levy (Honeydogs, Trailer Trash, Golden Smog)

Keyboardist of the Year: Tommy Barbarella (New Power Generation)

Horn Player of the Year: Brian Gallagher (Greazy Meal)

Female Vocalist of the Year: Laura Schlieske (Tina and the B-Side Movement)

Male Vocalist of the Year. Julius Collins (Greazy Meal)

Americana/Roots and Retro Group or Artist: Honeydogs

Americana/Roots and Retro Recording: Honeydogs, *Everything, I Bet You*

Blues Group or Artist: (tie) Willy Murphy and the Angel-Headed Hipsters and Jonny Lang and the Big Bang

Blues Recording: Mojo Buford, *Still Blowin' Strong*

Country Artist: Trailer Trash

Bluegrass Artist: Stoney Lonesome

Traditional and Modern Folk Artist: Spider John Koerner

Traditional and Modern Folk Recording: Cooker John, *Larry's Road Trip*

Jazz Group or Artist: Billy Franze Trio

Jazz Recording: Billy Franze Trio, *Live at MacKenzie*

Experimental/Instrumental/Environmental Recording: Glen Helgeson, *Spirit of the Wood*

Pop Group: Semisonic

Pop Recording: Semisonic, *Pleasure EP*

R&B Group or Artist: Greazy Meal

R&B Recording: Dr. Mambo's Combo, *Funkin' at the Bunker*

Gospel Group: Minneapolis Community College Choir

Hip-Hop Artist: Phull Surkle & Casino Royale

Hard Rock Group: Babes in Toyland

Modern Rock Group: Tribe of Millions

Overall Rock Recording: Balloon Guy, *The West Coast Shakes*

World Music Group or Artist: Eight Head

World Folk Group or Artist: Tim Sparks

Overall World Music Recording: Machinery Hill, *Whole Wide World*

Polka Band or Artist: The Wendlger Brothers

Local Music Radio Show: Mark Wheat, *Local Sound Dept.* (KFAI-FM)

Dance Artist or D.J.: Jezus Juice/Straight, No Chaser

Music Video: Babes in Toyland, "Sweet '69" (Phil Harder, Rick Fuller, directors)

Other Instrumentalist of the Year: Dave Boquist (Son Volt)

Children's Music Group: Teddy Bear Band

New Artist of the Year: The Dustbunnies

Producer/Engineer of the Year: Tom Herbers

Sound Person of the Year: Rob Curtis

Original Recording Compilation Album: *Minneapolis Does Denver*

Perpetually Outstanding Performer (male): Michael Bland (New Power Generation, Paul Westerberg)

Perpetually Outstanding Performer (female): Debbie Duncan

Connie Hector Award: Steve McClellan (First Avenue) ■

Ex-Prince Extravaganza

Tonight's Bash Celebrates the Release of the Three-disc *Emancipation* Set via Satellite TV and the Internet

November 12

WHEN THE ARTIST FORMERLY KNOWN AS PRINCE TAKES the stage at Paisley Park tonight at 11, it will be the mysterious Minneapolis superstar's highest-profile showcase since he threw The Beautiful Experience bash at Paisley in conjunction with the NBA All-Star Game in February 1994. But unlike that invitation-only party, which attracted such luminaries as Magic Johnson, David Robinson, Tony Robbins, Salt-N-Pepa, and Soul Asylum, tonight's audience figures to be considerably larger. Like, the world.

The concert, to celebrate TAFKAP's release from his Warner Bros. Records contract and his forthcoming three-CD set *Emancipation* (due in stores one week from today) is a by-invitation-only affair for friends, fans, and press, including representatives from the *New York Times, Los Angeles Times, Vibe, Rolling*

Stone, Entertainment Weekly, Us, Time, Billboard, Interview, and *Details.* But the concert also will be broadcast live via satellite, in keeping with the former Prince's longtime desire, which he articulated in a 1995 British television interview, to cut out the middle man: "In 1999, we'll be free and we can sell the music directly to the consumer. And we can give it away if we want."

"The show will be broadcast on any [television or radio] networks that want to, because it will be made available via satellite. But it's not an exclusive to anyone," said Maureen Coakley, publicist for EMI, the musician's new distribution company. "In keeping with the whole theme of *Emancipation,* he just wants it to be available. MTV and VH1 will be there, broadcasting from Paisley Park, but they're not going to get anything additional. They'll also just pick up on the satellite feed." Those with Internet capabilities will be able to access the performance in its entirety by logging on to the former Prince's website, The Dawn (www.thedawn.com). According to Coakley, the four-song showcase (and perhaps more) will be preceded by the world premiere of the video to TAFKAP's first single from *Emancipation,* a cover of the Stylistics' soul chestnut "Betcha by Golly, Wow." Of the clip, which was directed by TAFKAP and filmed at Paisley Park last week, Coakley said, "He thinks it's his most colorful video since [1985's] 'Raspberry Beret.' It's interesting. It's real positive. It's got fifty dancers in it, and Dominique Dawes from the U.S. Olympic [gymnastics] team is in it."

Today begins what Coakley characterizes as EMI's biggest marketing and promotion campaign ever. Bus shelter ads with the ex-Prince symbol and the word *Emancipation* already have sprung up. On November 19, when America Online subscribers log on to their computers, the screen will read "Emancipation Day." The former Prince traveled to Japan to meet with journalists, retailers, and broadcasters two weeks ago. He taped an interview with Oprah Winfrey last week at Paisley Park—which, along with a performance, will air November 21. He will headline the annual *Smash Hits* poll winners' party at London

Arena, which will be broadcast live on BBC1, on December 1. And next year, there are plans afoot for a worldwide tour.

Beyond the hype, how's the music? "It's really good," Coakley said. She went on:

> We had a few journalists here in New York up to hear it, and the buzz from that was that a lot of people were really impressed, and thought it sounded like old-school Prince, and sounded a lot better than stuff he's released in recent years. A lot of people here [at EMI] are big fans, certainly the president of the label and on down. I mean, they really feel secure that this is his best material in years. Everyone thinks that he's a huge talent, and because of lack of marketing, that he hasn't reached his potential. So with this big campaign, it's really putting him back to where he was.

No matter how good the grooves, or how aggressive the game plan, EMI has a monumental task at hand. While the former Prince's hard-core fans have remained loyal, and musicians almost uniformly respect his work, much of the world sees him as a sex-obsessed kook who changed his name to a symbol, wrote "Slave" on his face, and who now wishes to be referred to as "The Artist." Indeed, it may take more than a good record—not to mention a good marketing plan—to get people talking about the music again. "He's an enigma. That's part of why he's fabulous, right?" said Coakley. ∎

Stars Help Former Prince Celebrate His Freedom

November 13

HE'S FREE AT LAST. FLASHING HIS TRADEMARK LURID grin and vamping across the stage in a purple tunic, the Artist Formerly Known as Prince lit up the night at Paisley

Park in a star-studded gala performance Tuesday night. The half-hour show, broadcast live on cable channels, spotlighted TAFKAP's new three-CD set, *Emancipation,* in his debut performance with EMI, his new distribution company. It celebrates his release from his troubled Warner Bros. contract.

After a video clip of "Betcha by Golly, Wow," one of the songs on the new CD, the live show opened with dancers chanting, "Free at last, free at last. Thank God Almighty, we're free at last." Backed by the new four-piece version of his New Power Generation band, TAFKAP played five songs, including his famed "Purple Rain," and concluded the brief show with a cover of Joan Osborne's "One of Us." After a short news conference, TAFKAP returned to play more untelevised songs for the audience at Paisley Park. It was billed as the biggest musical event of the year and attracted show people from around the nation. Limousines and buses pulled up to the studios as local television news helicopters with infrared cameras tracked every warm body.

About an hour before the concert, TAFKAP and his wife, Mayte Garcia, walked from room to room and greeted people as a sea of fans followed them around. Some musicians on hand included members of Naughty by Nature and Boyz II Men. Minneapolis mayor Sharon Sayles Belton, St. Paul mayor Norm Coleman, and former Minnesota Twins star Kent Hrbek were among the local celebrities. The event smacked of a Hollywood gala as celebrities and mini-celebrities, most dressed to the nines, lined up at the various food tables and admired the others.

"The people watching has been good," Hrbek said as he stood with former Twins third baseman John Castino. Hrbek wore a gray suit and mock turtleneck, while Castino sported a generic baseball cap. Hrbek said his musical taste runs from polka to Frank Zappa. It wouldn't be a late night for him, he added. "Wednesday afternoon is my bowling day, so I have to get home at a reasonable hour," Hrbek said. ∎

♀ Speaks

November 17

OVER THE PAST THREE YEARS, WHENEVER I'VE REQUESTED an interview with the former Prince, he had said through his people—all of whom have since parted ways with him and his Chanhassen-based Paisley Park Studios—that he'd talk only when he was free from his contract with Warner Bros., his record label of the past seventeen years.

That day finally has arrived. Last month, ♀ inked a deal with the EMI–Capitol Records Group to distribute his albums on his own independent NPG label. And now that he's free at last, he's talking. In addition to last Tuesday's worldwide broadcast of the Paisley coming-out party for his three-CD set, *Emancipation*, TAFKAP has done a handful of select interviews, for *Rolling Stone, USA Today,* and the *Oprah Winfrey Show* (which airs Thursday).

When I arrive at Paisley last Monday, a woman is laying gold carpet in the foyer, in anticipation of the following night's gala. A bodyguard who could be on loan from the Chicago Bears' front four meets me at the door and directs me to the front desk. The walls are covered with gold and platinum records, and a new paint job is of billowy clouds on the stairwell leading up to the building's offices, with stars and planets on the ceiling. The woman behind the front desk whispers to the bear, "Have you seen the boss?" She disappears, and when she returns, she tells me, "He'll be with you in a minute." A few minutes pass, and TAFKAP strolls into the lobby with a good-natured, "Hey."

He's dressed in a sheer gray jumpsuit, draped with a black fishnet smock and several necklaces. "The zodiac stuff was Mayte's idea," he says, referring to Mayte Garcia, the singer's wife since February 1995. "It had to be more colorful."

He leads me into a small cluttered room on the first floor,

where an engineer is putting the finishing touches on "Betcha by Golly, Wow," the video for the first single from *Emancipation*. ♀ asks me if I have a tape recorder on me. I tell him that I brought one, just in case he has changed his practice of not allowing journalists to record his voice. "No way," he laughs. "Leave it in here."

The engineer cues up the clip, and ♀ is careful to let me know that it isn't finished—special effects of a rainbow and falling star will be matted in later today. And time is of the essence, for the video's world premiere on VH1, MTV, and BET is just thirty-three hours away. "I didn't have enough time," he says, "but I'm real proud of it."

We walk down a long corridor that houses several awards and is decorated with vintage Prince/♀ posters. I tell him the posters surprise me, since he has always been so tenacious about jettisoning his past. "I never look at these," he responds. "They're just for the kids when they come in here." He takes me on a short tour of the studio and into the huge soundstage room, where technicians and carpenters are busy putting together the set for the satellite simulcast of Tuesday's show.

He leads me into the control room of Studio B, where we settle into two swivel chairs behind the mammoth soundboard, which is decorated with two small decals of the symbol that is his new name. "Where's that tape recorder?" he says, more teasing than accusing. I pull it out of my bag and ask him where he wants it.

"In there," he replies, and I put it in a small closet that contains some recording equipment.

"Any more?" he asks. A little insulted, I say that no, I am not wired with a microphone and ask him if the no tape recorder rule stems from not wanting his voice out there.

"Yeah," he says. "I don't want it out there. You can call me paranoid, but . . . I mean, there's a picture disc of me back from '78 that's out there. You know, a kid tellin' stories."

The fact is, in his older age, ♀ has gotten better—there was a time when he wouldn't even allow journalists to use a pen and notepad. But when I ask him if that much is cool, he says, "Yes, yes—absolutely" and even provides me with a pencil. Cradled on his lap is the only copy of *Emancipation* that exists in the world at this point (the set will be released Tuesday). "I carry it with me wherever I go," he says, tapping on the jewel case. "It's like my little buddy."

The rapport between us is instantly easy, which surprises me. Over the twenty years I've spent covering, listening to, and dancing to Prince/♀, I developed a theory about his reluctance toward granting interviews. I assumed he simply wasn't verbal, and he relied on his two main modes of communication—sex and music—to express his feelings. Any interview, then, would likely consist of monosyllabic answers and cryptic asides. But the nearly two-hour interview proves to be exactly the contrary: he is very engaged, warm, smart, funny, deep, and extremely thoughtful.

His voice is not the slow, steady baritone of his stage banter, but an excited, animated burble. His eyes lock on mine whenever I ask him a question and, when answering, he either looks directly at me, stares out into the recording room, or twirls around in his chair. He responds to questions reflectively, confidently, curiously. The only other person I've been in a room with who exudes as much quiet energy and self-confidence is the cyclist Greg LeMond, who knew his body the way TAFKAP seems to know his muse and himself.

On the eve of what is arguably the biggest concert performance of his life, I ask him how much time we have. "How 'bout three minutes?" he sighs, a million odds and ends obviously weighing on him. I open my notebook and hope for a little longer.

Q: Whenever the name change is ridiculed, I always tell people that there were segments of society who ridiculed Cassius Clay when he changed his name to Muhammad

Ali. People change their names for religious reasons all the time, and for the most part people respect that. It seems strange, then, that people don't respect it when it happens for artistic reasons—and in your case, religious reasons.

A: Spiritual reasons, yeah. When I changed my name, I think I may have changed it too soon, because right now I feel that my change is just complete. And it was a different reason from what everyone thinks it was.

The Warner Bros. thing had very little to do with it. When I started writing "Slave" on my face, I did it because I had become a slave to myself. We don't know how we get here.

I had to figure out my origins and where I'm headed. How did I want the story to end? And I started writing "Slave" on my face because I felt like I was in a box spiritually, not creatively. You know, you can keep writing and writing, but that doesn't mean you're growing.

Q: Do you feel like you've grown spiritually?

A: Yeah. I don't think you ever stop growing spiritually, even if you feel like you have. But I had to do something. You know, R.E.M. can re-sign; I can re-sign; everybody can re-sign. But is that the way I want to progress? Can I take the route that I'm supposed to take? And during this time, I had to do the total recall, all the way back to '78 [the first Warner Bros. record, *For You*] and before. And all these people out there started speculating that "he's upset with himself," "he's upset with life," or "he's a brat." But that's not why I used the word *slave*. I was doing it as a reminder to myself.

It's a broad word. And by no means was I comparing myself to any people in any country—it's the concept of slavery. Look it up. And for me to write "Slave," what does that say about my oppressor? Who became my oppressor? That's what telepathy's about—finding the truth. Warner Bros. isn't the enemy. A man is his own enemy. They couldn't stop this [*Emancipation*]. They couldn't stop anything.

I didn't know where I was going ten years ago, but now I know where I'm going to be three thousand years from now.

Q: And where is that?

A: That's a secret.

Q: You say Warners isn't the enemy. How do you feel about them now?

A: Had I not gone there, I wouldn't be here now. I love Warner Bros. now. I know everyone thinks I'm nuts when I say that, but I love everyone in my past. I love them now. They had to be there for me to get to where I am now.

You've got to love humanity. We're put here to save one another—and it's hard to swallow, sometimes.

Q: So the "Slave" thing was a way of reminding you that you had to find a way out of your spiritual box?

A: When I went through this—and everybody goes through this—I was searching. Everybody has a path to his higher self, and what I named myself was my [vision] of my higher self. You can picture a perfect self; you can see your dream. And my higher self aspired to this [*Emancipation*].

And I had to go through everything I went through to get to this. And it's hard, because you get up every morning and write "Slave" on your face . . .

Q: Was there ever a time where you thought, "All right, already. I'm over this. I'm just not going to do it today."

A: Nope! No, no, no! Because you're not free. You don't feel free.

Q: This reminds me of something I read in a meditation book once: your twenties are about experimenting with who you are; your thirties are about becoming who you want to be; and your forties are about taking that self-knowledge out into the world. I suppose it's kind of that "Life begins at forty" philosophy—that if you do the work now, the rest of your days here can be extremely fruitful and gratifying. Is *Emancipation* the first time you've been aware of that path to what you call your higher self?

A: I saw it very clearly during [the making of] *1999* [in 1983]. Everything goes by very quickly. You can see time. I'm hearing the sound of a future time, and I'm listening to it in a car. You have to get that out of your head and onto the planet. After this [*Emancipation*], I don't feel the need [to make music] for a while. There won't be another record for a while. I feel like I could go to Hawaii and take a vacation.

Q: Have you ever felt that way before?

A: "When Doves Cry" and "Kiss." You go to a higher plane [of creativity] with that. They don't sound like anything else. "Kiss" doesn't sound like anything else. They aren't conscious efforts; you just have to get them out. They're gifts. Terence Trent D'Arby asked me where "Kiss" came from, and I have no idea. Nothing in it makes sense. Nothing! The high-hat doesn't make sense.

Q: What has fatherhood meant to you, creatively?

A: I don't know if I know yet. What I do know is that it makes me conscious of, more than anything, education. The first time I saw a person of color in a book, the person was hung from a tree. That was my introduction to African American history in this country. And again, going back to doing the total recall that I did, I know that that experience set a fire in me to be free.

You know that song "Let It Be"? There's a lot of heaviness in that song. We should pay attention to that. If I was in charge of the government, I would make it mandatory that at least once a year we have a Chill Day—where everybody just kicked back and watched. Everybody's so caught up in [the rat race] that we never really sit back and watch.

Q: You, of all people, seem to be in need of a Chill Day. You're so prolific, it's like you're working all the time. Haven't you ever wanted to take some time off, like other artists do, to let the muse percolate a little bit?

A: I don't work that way. I am music. I feel music. When I walk around, I hear brand new things. You're almost cursed. You're not even [its maker]: you're just there to bring it forth. You know, "Can't I go to sleep?" No. You can't. But okay, now you can. And you go to sleep, and you don't hear it, and then you're lonely. No one wants to be on Earth alone.

Q: How do you feel about how you've been portrayed in the media?

A: If people would go back and read in the newspaper all the things that have been written about me that weren't true, they'd know, and they could judge things for themselves.

I don't know what happened. The media has lost control. It's got too much power. What do these people think? That they're never going to see me again? That they're not going to want to come out here and see me face to face, or want to get into one of [the Pais-

ley events]? But it's all good. You see where I live. You
see what it's like. There's nothing wrong—there's never
been anything wrong. It's all our own destiny; we have
the key to it.

Q: Which brings us back to our search for the higher self.
What about people who have straight jobs, or who aren't
as creative?

A: Jim, we're all creative. I'm creative with music. You're
creative with your pen. The builders out there [working
on the soundstage] are creative with what they're building. Shoot, I couldn't do what they're doing. But if you
go sit down with them and interview them, they'll lay
some complex [stuff] on you, and their work is very, very
creative.

It takes everybody to do this. It even takes the person down the street to write the lies. It even takes *People* magazine, which said, "We'll put you on the cover if
we can have you, your wife, and your baby on it." Now, I
have been a musician for twenty years. This is the best
record I've ever made. You know: Kiss. My. Ass.

What time is it when people [value gossip more than
art]? But again, that gives me something to talk to you
about, and that gives us a joke that we can laugh about
here today. It's all connected.

Q: How did that search for higher self translate musically
on *Emancipation*?

A: There's a song called "In This Bed I Scream." We laid a guitar down on the floor of the studio and just recorded it.

There was electricity in the room, and sound. It just
depends on the energy coming out of the speakers and
the feedback. And we just let the groove take it and built
the song around the harmonics. You can hear the note,

and you can watch the colors blur. And right there, rules are already broken.

You know, there was a guy, a long time ago, who figured out you can get medicine out of mold. Think about that. "I'm going to eat this ugly green and moldy thing, and it will make me well." Which is just one way of God saying, "Everything I put on Earth can take care of you." And if you turn your back on that, if you turn your back on God, you turn your back on everything.

Did you see the interview after the [Evander] Holyfield fight? They were asking him how he beat Mike Tyson. And he was sitting there with his hat on that said "Jesus Is Love." And they just kept asking [Holyfield], and he kept talking about God. That he beat Tyson because of his faith in God.

But they didn't want to hear it. They were going, "Yeah, yeah, yeah, let's get off this God stuff. How'd you beat him?" And he's saying, "I'm telling you: it was God." Now will you tell me, what's his last name?

Q: Holy. Field.

A: Thank you. We're all down here to help one another. My best friends and worst enemies have had the same last name. If someone loves you, they hate you. People think week to week. They don't think about the big expanse.

I'm aspiring to my higher self, and the name I chose for myself, I wanted to represent freedom and truth and honesty.

Q: Over the past few years, you've slowly retreated to Paisley, doing shows here, recording here, working here, and not venturing out for surprise gigs the way you used to, at First Avenue and Glam Slam. Even though the gigs here have usually been pretty remarkable, I sometimes got the vibe that you were a caged rat in here, with not a lot of options to play out anywhere else. Did you ever feel that way?

A: No. Not at all. Not to start something, but when people say about me that I live in a prison and don't go anywhere, it's just not true. I go to the store, I go to the video store, I go to ballets, movies, the park. I live like anybody else. But I play music every day.

Now, I ain't talking about musicians who make a record, do a tour, and then chill for eight, nine months. This is my job. This [soundboard] is my desk. If that's a prison, then everybody else going to work is in a prison, too.

If you talk to people who have money, they'll tell you that money can't buy happiness. But it does pave the way for the search.

Q: What kind of advice would you give to that kid who started out doing this at Minneapolis Central High back in the '70s?

A: I could never give advice to myself. But I want to find out who the first person was who saw fit to sell music. Who came up with that concept? That's where the trouble started.

There's a bag of tricks [used by the music industry] that continue to work on people.

Take [R&B singer] D'Angelo. A very talented brother. Now, if I was a record executive, I'd do my best to get him to where I am now. Free. Letting it flow.

I just use D'Angelo as an example. But there's others. TLC—they're real nice people. What? When the record company gave them $75,000 and took $3 million, didn't they think TLC was gonna find out? Who's on the magazines and the websites and the records? Not the lawyers. Not the managers. Some artists need management. I don't. I can count.

And it all, always, comes back to God.

We are all down here to work toward one thing—love.

If I ain't got a ceiling over me, watch me fly. If I've got a ceiling over me, watch me rebel. You get enslaved to the bitterness. That's what the gangsta rap game is all about. All those records are being sold, but they're trapped in their own bitterness.

Q: On the tip of everybody aspiring to their higher self, what do you hope for the future?

A: One day all artists will be able to be part of an alternative music distribution setup, where there will be no limits. There will be no label president looking at his watch, saying, "Time's up! We need that record now." It's like with a painter. Would you ever say to a painter, "Oh, I'm sorry. We're running out of that color. You have to stop now."

If I was a journalist, I wouldn't write about something that wasn't positive. Like [Michael] Jordan. Phew. You can't criticize Jordan—ever. It's like Dre said [to a journalist]. You put some beats together. We'll sit here and wait. [He crosses his arms and taps his foot.] Can't do it? Okay, then take your pen and pad and get on down the road. [He bursts into laughter.] It's like with Jimmy [Jam] and Terry [Lewis]. They will never fall. They are the kings. I went to school with Jimmy. I know what he can do. He is a king. He is a king human being. And he is a good soul. Amen.

Oprah's another one. She's a queen. She was out here in the kitchen the other day. She's not like those other [talk show hosts]. She has chosen the high road. She's all about [positivity], and where's Jenny Jones? She's on trial, isn't she? Oprah is a queen. A queen.

And it's people like that that just [inspire] me. I talked to a radio deejay recently who told me that he got into deejaying because of me. He wanted to play my music. And that just knocked me back.

It was very, very emotional. And it just made me want to go and make another whole record. I've said the words in the past, "Welcome to the dawn," but I don't even know if I knew what they meant. Now I do.

It's the dawn of consciousness. If we all aspire to our higher selves, think of where it could go: universal knowledge. There. That's it. We'll end it on the highest note imaginable. ∎

Fresh (Ex-)Prince

Meet the New ♀, Same as the Old Prince: Lush, Warm, Funky, Effortless, Romantic, and in It for the Long Run

November 21

DEEP INTO THE THREE-CD, THREE-HOUR, THIRTY-SIX-song opus that is the Artist Formerly Known as Prince's *Emancipation,* there is a slow-burn funk track titled "Face Down." It lambastes a sucker gangsta rapper who embraced the glamorous thug life and now resides in a grave, "just like Elvis." ♀'s reference to Presley—pop music's most tragic casualty—takes on added irony here, considering that it comes from an artist whose own Elvisisms led one writer to describe him as "the Howard Hughes of rock." But *Emancipation* goes a long way toward dispelling the myth that ♀ is headed down the same path of such reclusive madmen as Presley and Hughes. Music is how ♀ connects and communicates with the world. When all is said and done, *Emancipation* is the sound of a musical genius taking control of his own destiny and subverting what the Fates have in store for him. Other artists, from Elvis to Mozart to Hemingway, have let their muses get the best of them in the latter stages of their careers, producing half-baked or inscrutable art that came off as either forced or feeble. But on *Emancipation* ♀ lets his muse flow freely.

None of the material here sounds labored over. Instead, it spills forth in a gush of aural brilliance that absolutely crackles off the laser. The most telling sign that this is the most effortlessly produced ♀ album to date is that he breaks many of his own rules, most notably Thou Shalt Not Record a Cover. *Emancipation* features four such tracks, including the cosmic reworking of Joan Osborne's "One of Us," and the effervescent first single, a remake of the Stylistics' 1972 hit "Betcha by Golly, Wow."

Unlike his last three albums (*Come, The Gold Experience,* and *Chaos & Disorder*), which combined old tracks from the vault and new (or, in the case of *Gold,* dated) material, the whole of *Emancipation* captures ♀ as he was, exactly, in 1996. bold, commercial, silly, freaky, and whipped-in-love. And though it's fairly impossible to absorb three hours of music in two or three listens, there are plenty of immediately recognizable high points. The party sounds that open "Jam of the Year" pay homage to Marvin Gaye's "After the Dance," while "Right Back Here in My Arms" and "Joint 2 Joint" (featuring KMOJ-FM deejay Michael Mac on vinyl scratches, a spoken-word segment by New York poet 99, and Savion Glover performing a tap dance interlude) sound like vintage club hits. The frisky "Courtin' Time" harkens back to the swing era (not to mention Prince's "Delirious"), and "Let's Have a Baby" is one of ♀'s best piano ballads. "The Human Body" is an irresistible techno-rave, "We

Gets Up" an NBA-arena staple waiting to happen, and ♀ even uncorks a couple of decent hip-hop workouts in the nasty "Face Down" and the cheeky bookends "Style" and "Mr. Happy."

The set's high point is the glorious "The Holy River," an affirmation of his spirituality that takes on a decidedly Eastern bent. The only drawback to *Emancipation* is that it doesn't encompass the kind of innovation that made Prince one of the most potent musical forces of the '80s, but that is also part of its charm. Like a handyman relying on his most trustworthy tools, ♀ builds an infrastructure of economical jazz, lush pop, romantic R&B, bubbly funk, and elegant ballads. And though Kate Bush, Rosie Gaines, Eric Leeds, and others contribute cameo performances, the lasting reaction to *Emancipation* is astonishment: that this wellspring of diverse sounds sprang from a single soul.

There are countless Elvises out there, collapsing under the weight of their self-myths. But *Emancipation* proves that ♀ isn't interested in such clichéd conclusions to his story. Like a great painter or composer who did his best work in his twilight, *Emancipation* is confirmation that ♀ will be making beautiful music into the next millennium—on his own terms. ∎

Ex-Prince Gives Royal Show at Paisley Park

Power Guitarists Show Strengths in TAFKAP's Band

December 30

THE TREES OUTSIDE PAISLEY PARK WERE DECKED OUT IN lights Saturday night. Inside was a huge Christmas tree, and the soundstage walls were decorated with white sheets and blinking lights.

"Happy holy days," the Artist Formerly Known as Prince told the gathering of approximately five hundred at the outset of a sixty-minute concert he gave with his band, the New Power Generation. Much of the audience comprised grade school and high school students (including several from the North Minneapolis–based visual arts school Juxtaposition Arts) who won trips to Paisley through radio stations from around the country.

Thanks to Chicago radio station V-100, many students came from Chicago, and TAFKAP chanted "Chicago in the house!" throughout much of his performance. Clad in a festive red shirt, red boots, black pants, and his trademark white parka emblazoned with the Prince symbol on the back, the former Prince opened the festivities with "The Jam of the Year," the first song off his latest three-CD opus *Emancipation*. The jam turned into a full-blown band revue that heavily featured the virtuosity of new guitarist Reverend Mike Scott. Next up was an extended version of James Brown's "Talkin' Loud and Sayin' Nothin'," for which the former Prince stood up at the piano and peeled off a litany of boogie-woogie runs and jazz riffs.

Despite several technical difficulties suffered by keyboardist Morris Hayes and drummer Kirk Johnson, the performance served as a much more revealing showcase of the New Power Generation than the November 12 worldwide *Emancipation* broadcast. This band is a jazzier, more full-bodied outfit than the previous version of the NPG, and what they lack in power they make up for in finesse. Nasty bassist Kathleen Dyson is the group's defining secret weapon, along with the fact that after the former Prince has handled all the guitar chores himself over the past few years, now the NPG features three formidable ax killers (TAFKAP, Scott, and Rhonda Smith), all of whom proved to be spectacular rhythm and lead players.

For many in the audience Saturday night, the highlights of the nine-song set were the oldies ("Purple Rain," "17 Days," "The Most Beautiful Girl in the World," "The Cross"), but the

most exuberant moments came with the *Emancipation* material: during "Get Yo Groove On," the former Prince pranced
out onto the catwalk and grinned sheepishly when he lost his
place and forgot his own lyrics. For "Face Down," a sampled
voice burped, "Dead like Elvis," and TAFKAP strapped on the
bass, coaxing an extraordinary array of climbs and solos from
the instrument. Also noteworthy was a piano cameo from R&B
star Tony Rich.

The finale was a cover of Joan Osborne's "One of Us," which
the former Prince introduced as "a damn good song for all of
us—people of all races, all denominations, all love." Some critics have wondered why TAFKAP covered Osborne's omnipresent hit of last year on *Emancipation*. But watching him perform
it with such passion, it was abundantly clear: it is a thundering
proclamation of his faith and a testament to the mysteries of
faith. When he sang it Saturday night, it turned Paisley Park
into a rock 'n' soul church where the homily goes "God is great,
God is good, Yeah, yeah, yeah, yeah, yeaaaah."

After the service, the former Prince and his wife, Mayte, clad
in matching white silk outfits, met with students in a back
room. Some of the kids asked questions about where he went
to school and about his CD. But when a few asked for autographs, he laughed and said, "We can do better that that," and
presented everyone with black parkas with the Prince symbol
on the back. ∎

1997

Prolific Ex-Prince Working on
Next Album, *The Truth*

D URING HIS INTERVIEW WITH THE ARTIST FORMERLY
Known as Prince on VH1 last weekend, Chris Rock asked,
"When you were at Warner Bros., you took a lot of flack for putting out too many albums. Do you ever feel that if you were an
artist in another time period that you'd be more appreciated? I
mean, Mozart or Beethoven probably put out the equivalent of
an album every month."

Midway through the question, the former Prince nodded
his head as if it wasn't the first time he'd considered the notion, then answered: "Aretha Franklin every three months had
a new album. James Brown every three months had a new single and album. Yeah, if I had been in that time period . . ." He
never finished the thought, but in other recent interviews, the
former Prince has said that his goal is to "have the biggest section in the record store—the most titles" and to "write a song
a day for the rest of my life." In November, the week before the
release of the Chanhassen-based musician's three-hour, thirty-
six-song epic *Emancipation*, the former Prince told the *Pioneer
Press* that the *Emancipation* project had proven to be hugely
satisfying. So much so that for the first time in his life after
making a record, he felt he could take a vacation.

Vacation over.

Late last week, Paisley Park sent out a test-pressing CD of
two new songs to a select group of friends, journalists, and
deejays. Included in the package was a card commemorating
Valentine's Day, which marks the one-year anniversary of the
former Prince's wedding to his former dancer/backup singer,
Mayte Garcia-Nelson. (Word is that the couple will celebrate

with a series of concerts in Honolulu over the weekend.) The two new tracks are "The Truth" and "Don't Play Me." And while the compositions are typically marvelous, the (pending?) release isn't exactly stop-the-presses news, since the prolific musician obviously doesn't suffer from writer's block. But one thing makes these songs different and therefore newsworthy: both are stripped-down acoustic numbers peppered with ambient noise. A notation on the back of the CD's handcrafted jewel box reads, "From the 4thcoming acoustic recording 'The Truth.'"

One of the most oft-repeated criticisms of *Emancipation* was that although it exhibited a new depth of lyrical spirituality it didn't break much new musical ground, and many of the tracks were haunted by echoes of Prince's commercial heyday. But if these two fresh, decidedly noncommercial recordings are any indication, the former Prince is about to deliver the acoustic work that his fans have long been clamoring for. The only question is, Where will it turn up? *Emancipation* was released on the former Prince's New Power Generation Records and distributed by the EMI–Capitol Records Music Group. Both artist and label have stressed that in terms of marketing, *Emancipation* is a two-year project and that sales depend on the Fecund One's ability to rein in his muse to concentrate on promoting the project at hand, such as his two latest singles, "Somebody's Somebody" and "The Holy River."

Therefore, to avoid competing with his own albums, the logical outlet for "The Truth" is the on-again, off-again 1-800-New-Funk mail-order service, which currently sells *Kamasutra*, a full-length ballet composed in collaboration with Mayte, and an official bootleg of the January 11 concert at the Roseland Ballroom in New York. Also scheduled to drop via mail order in the near future is *Crystal Ball*, a three-CD set of previously bootlegged material.

Most music superstars release one album every two years. Not the former Prince. One critic referred to such activity as his "creative diarrhea." But while it may be difficult for the mainstream music industry to keep track of, his method (write, re-cord, release) is not unlike, if you will, that of a daily newspaper columnist.

Once upon a time, the former Prince wanted to buck the major label system. Now he's doing it—and that's *The Truth*. ■

Singing Vegan Praises

June 25

CALL HIM THE ARTIST FORMERLY KNOWN AS A CARNI-vore. On the ex Prince's last album, the Minneapolis super-star confessed to the world that his favorite breakfast cereal is "Cap'n Crunch—with soy milk, because cows are for calves." His forthcoming album, *The Truth*, features the song "Animal Kingdom," in which he admonishes a friend (Spike Lee?) for appearing in pro-milk advertisements; declares that he doesn't "eat red meat, white fish, or that funky funky blue cheese"; and pledges to live in harmony with his "brothers and sisters in the sea."

According to sources close to the Artist, the thirty-nine-year-old musician recently bought a farm near his Chanhas-sen home, and his wife, Mayte, cooks all their meals—strictly vegan, an outgrowth of vegetarianism that forbids consump-tion of meat, eggs, or dairy products. It is all part of a spiritual awakening that the former Prince has undergone in the past few years.

Here in the Twin Cities, there is a growing vegan-band movement. In addition to the Artist, many punk and ska bands feature vegan members. Lyrics, fanzines, and whole songs are devoted to the lifestyle, and one group, the up-and-coming Minneapolis-based hard-core punk band I Shot McKinley, is made up of four vegans: Adam Patterson (drums), Mike Peterson (bass), Eric Graham (singer), and Mike Browning (guitar). All are between nineteen and twenty years old, have been vegans for about two years, and became vegans primarily for ethical and animal rights reasons, but acknowledge the health and environmental benefits. They wear no leather, suede, silk, or wool and use only cruelty-free products. None of the four is in school at the moment (Patterson is taking correspondence courses from the American Holistic College of Nutrition), and all but Browning are employed. But he and Peterson, who both have restaurant experience, dream of one day opening the first vegan café in the Twin Cities.

"Ninety-five percent of the people involved in the punk scene are at least vegetarian, and animal rights is a pretty common issue that's addressed in the songs," says Peterson, sitting in the sun room of the sparsely furnished house he shares with Patterson and Browning in the Whittier neighborhood of Minneapolis. Graham, the singer, has influenced several people to go vegan or vegetarian. Even his parents are trying. "It's hard because they've been in this [other] lifestyle for forty-something years," Graham says. "But my mom's just drinking soy milk now, and my dad will only eat white meat."

I Shot McKinley wants to change the world. According to Patterson, much of the vegan–hard-core connection can be traced back to Minor Threat, the seminal Washington, D.C.–based band whose 1981 song "Straight Edge" was a call for members of the hard-core scene to abstain from drugs and booze. "You'll find it very common that most people who are vegan don't drink, do drugs, or smoke, because they're health conscious," Peterson adds.

Maintaining the vegan lifestyle isn't difficult. Local supermarkets now stock plenty of grains, legumes, nuts, soy products, and a variety of fruits and vegetables. And such places as Aveda, the Body Shop, and Restore the Earth carry cleaning and grooming products (toothpaste, soap, shampoo, etc.) that are biodegradable, cruelty-free, and nontoxic. The four band members consider veganism a lifetime commitment, and they want others to consider it, too. "Getting our message out to people about veganism through our music can kind of make us feel less guilty about our wasteful human lifestyles," Patterson says.

Message sent. Are there any more?

"Can you introduce us to Prince?" Graham asks.

"Yeah," Patterson says. "That would be awesome." ∎

The Artist Will Play Sayles Belton Benefit Show

September 10

TONIGHT THE ARTIST FORMERLY KNOWN AS PRINCE and his band, the New Power Generation, will play at a fund-raising concert for Minneapolis mayor Sharon Sayles Belton. The show, scheduled to begin after doors open at 8 P.M., will be at Paisley Park Studios in Chanhassen. Tickets are $100 per head—a rather higher cover charge than the free admission for the one-hour-and-forty-five-minute show last Friday night/Saturday morning.

This isn't the first time the Artist has funked for Her Honor. On January 14, 1995, he staged another pricey party that drew six hundred well-heeled politicos and society types in gowns and tuxes. That night, the lovefest between the mayor and the musician was obvious. Sayles Belton introduced the former Prince as "the greatest musician in the world, a man who put Minnesota on the map." During his sixty-five-minute set, he returned the favor, commenting, "1994 was a strange one. Are we glad it's gone? Yeah. There was one nice thing that happened last year. I made one friend. She goes by the name of Sharon Sayles Belton."

More recently, the Artist has been on an East Coast tour and received a rave live review in the new issue of *Rolling Stone* magazine. He will also make an appearance on HBO's *Muppets Tonight* TV show on Sunday. ■

For TAFKAP Fans, It Was All Simply in the Line of Duty

December 5

RICK OLSON ARRIVED AT TARGET CENTER LAST FRIDAY afternoon at 3 P.M. He set up camp outside the farthest door leading to the arena lobby with a sleeping bag, blanket, and headphones. Not long after, the twenty-seven-year-old Coon Rapids resident was joined by a couple of strangers—Heidi Butler, a twenty-seven-year-old student teacher from St. Paul, and her friend, Julie Spence. "We're fanatics," said Olson.

As the afternoon became the evening, more campers—black and white, young and older—settled in behind the trio, and a line began to form. By midnight, the line was all the way down First Avenue. By 8:30 Saturday morning, it was curling its way around North Seventh Street and providing a concrete answer to the question of just how popular the Artist Formerly Known as Prince's first concert at Target Center on December 10 would be. At 9 A.M., the doors opened, and forty-eight hours later all fifteen thousand tickets would be gone, necessitating a second show December 11. Those tickets went on sale this past Wednesday, and the scene at Target Center was repeated.

"Our last sellout was Fleetwood Mac, but that took a few weeks," said Target Center's Karen Fine. "Everybody's interested in this one." Especially everybody who lay out on the cold sidewalk overnight for something they could have secured simply by dialing a phone number. That's what the majority of ticket buyers did: 1-989-REDIAL. The rest bundled up against the cold, huddled next to their neighbor, played Prince/Artist tapes on their boom boxes, and had a big ol' slumber party.

Some came after they got off work Friday night. Some got in line after seeing the Semisonic show at First Avenue. Some woke up early Saturday morning and came down. Some got in line and had friends save their place as they went out to Paisley Park in Chanhassen, where the former Prince was holding a dance party, and came back to report the doings. Throughout the night, they saw a pretty nasty car accident in front of Target Center. A few campers built a bonfire that the cops eventually made them douse. When asked why they were out there, when the rest of the world was tucked away in bed, almost everyone said, "For the experience." What they didn't say is that it was a chance to bond with a group of people who feel on the outs with a general populace that has decided their nameless hero is a freakazoid, or old news. "People like that aren't really listening to the music," said Butler. "They're more focusing on the publicity, the strange things they think he does. And if they listen to the music, it's a totally different story. That's the true source."

Butler has been a Prince fan since she was in fifth grade and first heard "Purple Rain" in 1984. At that time, her parents forbade her to go to any of the five sold-out *Purple Rain* concerts at the St. Paul Civic Center. "I've been making up for it ever since," she said. "That's why I spent the night here. Blame my parents." Like many of her fellow campers, Butler has made several treks to Paisley Park, where the Artist has frequently performed over the past two years. Earlier this year, she and Spence traveled to Denver to catch one of the first Jam of the Year tour dates. "This is kind of torturous, because you have to go when he plays here," said Butler, nodding up at the basketball arena's outer facade. "But you don't really want to, because the whole world comes when he comes out in public."

Jon Copeland, a longtime Minneapolis music supporter and

KFAI deejay sees it slightly differently. "I feel very lucky to have seen him at Paisley so many times, to have been able to go out there and just see him in such a small atmosphere," said Copeland, who stood midway down the line. "But it will be fun to see him do a big arena show, too. I like to have both worlds."

That duality is also part of the charm of the line. For every die-hard disciple clad in a New Power Generation jacket and matching hat, for every savvy enthusiast tapped into the Paisley underground, for every bootlegger completist, there are dozens of campers who have never seen a single show by the musician who is widely regarded as the greatest live performer of his generation. "It's been a lifetime goal to see him," said eighteen-year-old Georgia native Melissa Washington, a student at the University of Minnesota standing near the back of the line with her friend, twenty-two-year-old Jemika Hayes. "I've been waiting for this moment forever," said Hayes, a musician/songwriter who works at JCPenney at Southdale. "He plays a lot, but it's hard to know when, because it's really unannounced. You never hear about it until the day after."

Several campers said that they haven't listened to much of the former Prince's '90s output, with the exception of last year's three-CD set, *Emancipation*. Most sheepishly admitted that they hoped he would perform old hits like "Purple Rain." But the majority said the reason they have remained loyal while so many have jumped off the purple bandwagon is that he possesses an insatiable appetite for musical envelope pushing. "He constantly experiments, which is why I think we're all still interested in him," said James Walsh (no relation), who was standing in line with his sister, Kelly. "He's daring, and we all want to listen to someone who's a little daring. If he was like [the band] Chicago, I mean, who wants to listen to that again? We've already heard it. Who can wake up in the morning and say, 'We've already heard Prince'? You can't, because you don't know what's coming next."

Around 8 A.M., the crowd packed up lawn chairs, sleeping

bags, coolers, boom boxes, and portable TVs, and hauled them to their cars. When the doors opened at 9 A.M., there was a rush to the door, but order was instantly restored by Target Center security guards. Olson, Butler, and Spence were directed to the farthest windows of the Target Center box office. But the tellers at the windows were too slow ("They're training them in or something," said an exasperated Butler), and campers who had stood behind them were awarded front-row seats. Olson, who was first in line, had hoped to secure not good seats but great ones. Front row center, to be exact. He got sixteenth row. After spending eighteen hours in line, was he disappointed? "Not really, because it was a great time. We became a pretty close-knit group up there. And it's going to be a great show." ■

Jammin'

For His First Local Area Gig in Years, the Artist
Is Stripped Down and Bare-wired . . . and
Reports from the Road Say He's Back on Top
of the Game

December 7

THE ARTIST'S JAM OF THE YEAR TOUR STARTED IN JULY, and since then reports from the road have been ridiculously positive.

And why not? In the '80s, Prince was one of the greatest concert draws of the decade, thanks to his outlandish, playful, and supremely funky stage shows. These days, all the frills are gone, and the focus is exclusively on the music. The set is decidedly bare-bones, and that's how it should be: he comes from an old school of musicians who grew up valuing live performance, whereas too many hip-hop/alternative rock/R&B musicians now consider live gigs to be a distant third priority, after making records and videos. As Neil Strauss of the *New York Times* wrote after catching one of the first Jam of the Year shows: "In 2-1/2 hours, the Artist made it clear what low standards we've set for rock and pop concerts in the '90s. Instead of trying to replicate his albums, he tore apart his meticulous pop songs and turned them into long, organic, captivating jams."

So get ready, 'cause here he comes. In addition to playing material from last year's three-disc opus, *Emancipation,* the little purple love god has been dipping into the Prince catalog for such hits as "Purple Rain," "1999," and "Raspberry Beret." Here's hoping we'll also hear cuts from his forthcoming albums, *Crystal Ball* and *The Truth.*

Wednesday and Thursday's shows are the former Prince's first arena concerts since an impromptu rehearsal for the *Nude* tour at the St. Paul Civic Center in 1991, and the first advertised arena concerts since he kicked off the *Lovesexy* tour in 1988 at the Met Center. Opening the show will be Larry Graham, the former bassist and vocalist for Sly & the Family Stone and Graham Central Station. Arrive early, since the Artist and Graham have been engaging in some reportedly roof-raising jams during Graham Central's warm-up. ∎

Sticking to the Fax

Ex-Prince speaks (sort of) in an interview on the eve
of his two Target Center shows

December 10

TO PROMOTE HIS JAM OF THE YEAR TOUR, WHICH VISITS Target Center this week, the Artist Formerly Known as Prince is granting interviews—via fax.

So I whipped up thirty-two questions—including a couple about the long-awaited, long-delayed, mail-order-only release

of his massive new compilation, *Crystal Ball,* and its compan-
ion acoustic album *The Truth*—and faxed them off to his offices in Paisley Park in Chanhassen, where this week the Artist
has been busy recording Chaka Khan and Larry Graham—two
old-school funkateers who have served as opening act for
many of the Jam tour dates.

What he faxed back is the following (answering twenty-one
of thirty-two), verbatim, complete with computer graphic–
generated eye-icons for the word *I,* numbers for words, and
other cryptic characters that the pop world has come to asso-
ciate with the one-and-only Artist:

1. Where are you doing this interview? What time is it?

   A: 👁'm in my skin. It's ten minutes 2 Armageddon.

2. I talked to a lot of your fans who were standing in line
   for tickets at the Target Center the other day, and several wanted to know when *Crystal Ball* will be out. What
   stage is it at? When will it be available?

   A: It is being pressed. By Xmas, shipping will start. It is
   well worth the wait.

3. When you're not on the road, do you spend a lot of time
   on your computer? What kind of a computer do you
   have?

   A: 👁 have a Compaq given 2 me by some friends at Micro-
   soft. Because of my work with Larry & Chaka, 👁 haven't
   had much time recently 4 anything other than funk.

4. Who or what inspires you these days?

   A: My constant source of inspiration is God.

5. The Jam of the Year tour has been getting great reviews.
   You come from an old school of musicians who grew up
   valuing live performance. Not a lot of bands bring it like

you do. Do you sense that people are starved for the sort of real spontaneity and fan-musician connection that you provide?

A: They're definitely starved, and 👁 am the chef!

6. For you, what is the biggest difference between performing live now and when you were touring nonstop in the '80s?

A: Nothing. As 1999 approaches—many of my songs become more relevant.

7. Most of the time after an arena concert, you'll perform at a late-night aftershow at a club. Where do you get all the energy?

A: Same answer as #4.

8. What are you reading at the moment?

A: The Bible.

9. Have you ever felt like you've repeated yourself, musically?

A: Of all the ?s! 👁've written over a thousand melodies, so if 👁 have—no big deal! :)

10. You're always attempting to challenge yourself in different ways. You never coast; you're always pushing. Where does that drive come from?

A: Same answer as #7.

11. What is the longest time away from the studio/guitar/ stage you've ever spent? How did it feel?

A: 👁've blanked out such memories. 👁've had 2 enter Studio Rehab two times in ten years. Change the subject.

12. These days, you're functioning like an independent label owner. You've expressed your admiration for people
like Eddie Vedder and Ani DiFranco. Who else do you
admire, business-wise?

A: Michael Jordan.

13. Now that you're also an independent tour promoter, do
you find that being more involved with that takes time
and energy away from your creativity?

A: Here's how U promote a concert—take out an ad
in the paper, call the radio stations and give them the
ticket price & the date, then just show up. How much energy is required for that? Yet another Rock 'n' Roll myth.

14. "Circle of Amour" from *The Truth* mentions four friends
from your old high school, Minneapolis Central. Who
are they, and what inspired you to write a song about
them?

A: Are you trying 2 get me in2 a lawsuit? It's a fictional
story!

15. I went to your high school reunion last year and talked to
a couple of your old teachers. Bea Hasselmann, who was
the music teacher at Central, said, "In my opinion, that
'71-'81 Central was the most peacefully integrated school
in the history of the state. I don't know what happened."
To me, that speaks to a lot of what your music has always been about—freedom, racial harmony, positivity,
and pride. Your old teachers spoke wistfully about those
days, since in many ways we've gone backwards as a society. Does that bother you, as well? And do your years
at Central continue to inspire you to write about race?

A: The state of race relations affects me more than ever
now that ◉ run my own affairs. Londell McMillan—my

attorney—is involved in a lawsuit where a record executive made a remark that went something like this—
"If we (meaning the music industry) didn't hire people
with criminal records, there would be no Blacks in the
music business." Hmmm.

16. Of all of the bands you've had, what has been your favorite to play with, in terms of generating live heat?

    A: ◉ don't set foot onstage unless it's hot. ◉'m not a
    judge.

17. After a long period of never playing Prince material,
you're back to performing old stuff—even "Purple Rain."
How does that feel now?

    A: Like home. These songs r like my children and ◉ love
    every one of them.

18. Most members of the "other side" of the Minneapolis
Sound, from Soul Asylum's Dave Pirner, the Replacements' Paul Westerberg, and Trip Shakespeare/Semi-
sonic's Dan Wilson, have acknowledged your influence
on them over the years, but you've never commented on
how that part of the Minneapolis Sound impacted you.
Did it? Have you paid attention to that stuff over the
years?

    A: Same answer as #10.

19. You tend to fire people, and/or people come and go
pretty regularly. How does that feel, karma-wise? Does
it bother you that you have a number of people out there
who you were once close to, but to whom you now never
speak?

    A: My address is the same. They just never show up. The
    people who pay return visits r the ones who really love
    me, not the pretenders.

20. Any chance that you'll perform at First Avenue anytime soon?

A: If they ask, 👁'd be glad 2.

21. What are five songs you wish you'd written?

A: 👁 did write them—"Sign o' the Times," "Gold," "Purple Rain," "Little Red Corvette," "The Holy River." ■

Pure Artist-ry

The Former Prince Puts Aside All Faux Stage
Trickery and Delivers Just Pure, Organic,
Funky, Fabulous Music

December 11

"**D**ID YOU MISS ME?" THE ARTIST FORMERLY KNOWN as Prince asked his hometown during a cover of James Brown's "Talkin' Loud and Saying Nothin'" at the outset of the first of his two Target Center concerts Wednesday night. "Well, I missed you, too. Let's see if we can make up for it to-night." That he did, with a mind-blowing, two-hour-plus revue of greatest hits, new jams, hard funk, and scintillating, sexy, searing showmanship that will stand as one of the most—if not the most—memorable live music shows ever hosted at the big basketball arena.

Got a ticket for tonight? Good. No? Then, my friend, you are a fool.

Before Wednesday night, the last time the man born Prince Rogers Nelson had performed at an advertised arena concert in Minneapolis was September 14, 1988. That night, a throng at the Met Center witnessed the opening leg of the North American *Lovesexy* tour, and what a party it was. As one of the biggest recording stars of the '80s, Prince entered the sold-out Met in a '67 white Thunderbird, a cheeky bit of excess that set the tone for the evening. Throughout that two-and-a-half-hour show, the little nymph pranced around the garish set, playfully shooting baskets at a hoop, acting out sexual and spiritual passion plays, and engaging in faux lovers' quarrels with his backup dancer Cat and drummer Sheila E.

A lot has changed over the past nine years. Prince is no longer Prince but an unpronounceable symbol; he no longer records for his record label of sixteen years, Warner Bros.; and as a result he has lost some of his pop star cache. Something else has changed as well. In the '80s, rock, pop, funk, and hip-hop still were considered rebel music. But in the '90s, the power of music has been co-opted to the point at which it's hard to tell the real deal from the quasi-cool Gap jingles. And seemingly single-handedly, the ex-Prince has set out to reclaim music as something powerful, special, and transformational.

Wednesday night the most ostentatious stage ornamentations were some gold planets aligned over the stage, a giant ⚥ backdrop, and some gold lamé lionesses flanking both sides of the stage. There were no big video screens or any of the other modern-day concert tics to hold a crowd's hand—just pure, organic, funky, fabulous music.

The night started off with a rousing set by former Sly & the Family Stone vocalist Larry Graham and his group, Graham Central Station. Over the course of forty minutes, Graham's crew pumped out some of the '60s and '70s most memorable soul hits, including "Family Affair," "Thank You Falettinme Be Mice Elf Agin," "Dance to the Music," "Everyday People," and "Wanna Take You Higher." When GCS left the stage, it was hard not to wonder how the former Prince would top that.

But top it he did. And considering the amount of amazing material he's written over the past twenty years, the thirty-nine-year-old master did well to placate fans of all denominations. He dipped into his back catalog for old treasures, including full performances and/or snippets of "Kiss," "I Would Die 4 U," "When Doves Cry," "Little Red Corvette," "I Could Never Take the Place of Your Man," "The Cross," "Sexy M.F.," "If I Was Your Girlfriend," "Darling Nikki," "Diamonds and Pearls," "Take Me with U," and "Raspberry Beret." He crooned a breathy, heartbreaking reading of "How Come U Don't Call Me Anymore?," dry-humped the piano during "Delirious," uncorked a screaming guitar solo during "Purple Rain," and midway through the set performed a version of "Do Me, Baby" that was so perfectly erotic it should be packaged and sold to infertility clinics across the land. (Call 1-800-NEW-FETUS.)

But the highlight of the night was a new song, the monster "Face Down," from the former Prince's *Emancipation* album of last year. As the band cranked up, he instructed parents to take their kids out into the lobby to avoid the "harsh language." From there, the New Power Generation (guitarists Mike Scott and Rhonda Smith, keyboardist Morris Hayes, bassist Kathleen Dyson, drummer Kirk Johnson) proved to be the tightest, hardest-working band currently on the road. Only their funky leader worked harder, playing guitar, portable keyboard, bass, and piano. And finally, there was this: fifteen thousand people on their feet as the clock moved well past midnight, hollering in unison, "Tonight we're gonna party like it's 1999."

That's when it hit me. How long have we been singing that? Actually, it's been exactly fifteen years. Even when we haven't been singing it, we've been singing it. It's become a part of our collective consciousness, and last night at the Target Center it felt like a mass lighting of a very long firecracker fuse, set to go off next year as the countdown to the millennium commences.

But before all that jazz, the party continues tonight. Be there or be foolish. ∎

The Artist Wears 'Em Out at Post-concert Paisley Park Party

December 12

THE BASKETBALL PRESS BOX AT THE TARGET CENTER IS high above the arena's nosebleed seats. I arrived there around 7:30 P.M. Wednesday and proceeded to set up my portable computer and do a bit of preparation for my review of the first of Prince's two homecoming shows. There was nobody else in the house, save for a few security people and what I assumed was the warm-up act onstage, running through a late sound check. But in fact what I saw was a scene that would convince even the staunchest Prince detractor that he is by no means an above-it-all superstar and that his concern is first and foremost music. There he was, in an empty arena, with thousands outside waiting to be let into the Target Center, conducting a sound check with the opening act, former Sly & the Family Stone singer/bassist Larry Graham and his band, Graham Central Station. The former Prince was acting as part cheerleader, part technician, testing microphones and getting funky in a low-burn sort of way.

That was the first time I laid eyes on him Wednesday night. The last time was nine hours later, as he stood on a stairwell at Paisley Park in Chanhassen, his hands clapping wildly and his body convulsing as Graham led a thinned-out crowd of die-hards in a chorus of "I Wanna Take You Higher." What happened in between was probably the most amazing night of music I have ever witnessed.

If you were there, or if you read Thursday's paper, you know that Graham and the former Prince blew the roof off the Target Center Wednesday. But as it turns out, the night was just getting started. As the crowd headed for the turnstiles, a voice boomed out over the P.A., informing the already rung-out throng that "the aftershow party is at Paisley Park." Which is where about five hundred fanatics trekked to. At 2:30 A.M., the former Prince and the New Power Generation (guitarists Mike Scott and Rhonda Smith, keyboardist Morris Hayes, bassist Kathleen Dyson, drummer Kirk Johnson) took to the tiny stage in the studio's small disco. They played a loose, nasty, eighty-five-minute set that included scorching versions of Sly's "I'll Take You There" and Rufus's "You Got the Love," both featuring the sublime lead vocal talents of Smith. And during the supremely bad "Days of Wild," KMSP-TV anchor Robyne Robinson got up onstage and shook her sassy, classy booty.

It was that kind of night, where people threw caution to the wind and seized the moment. My review had already been written for the night, so I had left my notebook in the car. But as things heated up, I was looking for scraps of anything to write on. The *Strib*'s Jon Bream was doing the same thing. We were searching for notebooks and adjectives. I found a reasonable facsimile of the former (a ticket envelope), but to my knowledge they haven't invented the latter yet.

After the jam, in the lobby, I asked Hayes if they were going to play again. He was wearing his coat and hat and looked like he was ready for bed. "I don't know, man. I hope not." Johnson said the same thing and added with a wan grin, "It's not like we've got a show to play tomorrow [Thursday] night, or anything."

Meanwhile, their fearless funky leader was scooting around the place, talking to fans and friends, bouncing to the recorded music and obviously imbued with the magic of the moment. Sure enough, at 4:20 A.M., an amalgamation of GCS and the NPG hit the stage again and delivered a stunning forty-minute sampling of soul nuggets, including the Isley Brothers' "Shout" and Jackie Wilson's "Lonely Teardrops." Understand, all this came after a ridiculously energetic two-and-a-half-hour concert that would have killed most other performers. This is what I scribbled on my ticket envelope: "Stamina? He is not human. He is a freak of nature. Jordan. Lung capacity."

Indeed, by the time he performed the evening's closer, "1999," at the Target Center, there were probably nine thousand left (out of a sold-out fifteen thousand), because he had simply worn them out. The Paisley show started with a count of five hundred, but when it was done, there were only 150 left standing.

One onlooker suggested that the guy's great endurance can be credited to Revive, a trendy new energy drink. My guess is that it is the power of the funk and something he said when I interviewed him last November. Naïvely, I asked if he ever felt a need to take time off so that his muse could percolate. "I don't work that way," he said, sitting in his studio. "I am music. I feel music. When I walk around, I hear brand new things. You're almost cursed. You're not even [its maker]: you're just there to bring it forth. You know, 'Can't I go to sleep?' No. You can't." ■

1998

Grand Funk Express

Larry Graham, the Man Who Invented Funk,
Pulls His Graham Central Station into a New
Chanhassen Terminal

April 19

W HEN CHANHASSEN'S FOUNDING FATHERS ESTAB-
lished the Minneapolis suburb in 1852, they chris-
tened their little hamlet on the prairie with a name derived
from *Chanhassan*, the Dakota Indian word for "the tree with
sweet sap." Chanhassen's first settlers were farmers and rail-
road workers. Little did they know that some 150 years later,
their great-grandchildren's neighbors would be two pioneers
of funk.

Chanhassen's most famous funk father is Prince, who has
based his musical and business operations out of his Paisley
Park Studios there since the '80s. The newest resident is fif-
ty-one-year-old bassist/singer Larry Graham, who, along with
his wife of twenty-three years, Tina, and their fifteen-year-old
daughter, Latia, moved into a modest modern bungalow near
Paisley Park two weeks ago. And while Prince is now known as
the Artist Formerly Known as Prince, it is no exaggeration to
designate Graham as the Man Who Invented Funk.

"A lot of people have said that. All I can say is, 'Thank you,'"
says Graham, a warm, gentle man who greeted his visitor with
a handshake and a bear hug. The equally genial Tina sits at
his side on a plush leather love seat, nodding enthusiastically
at the assertion that her husband's distinctive bass playing,
which first funked the world with Sly and the Family Stone
in the late '60s, is the seminal ingredient that launched funk.

Even if the Man Who Invented Funk won't come out and
say as much, the Grahams' lushly carpeted basement says oth-

105

erwise. A pool table sits in the middle of the room, flanked by a bank of keyboards, speakers, a giant TV and stereo system, and the sort of wall decorations that would make drooling fools out of the curators of the new Hard Rock Cafe rumored to be opening on Hennepin Avenue in Minneapolis later this year.

An oil portrait of a Sly-era Graham, an awfully '70s painting of cartoon dancers doing the Freddy to his band, Graham Central Station, adorns the wall, along with a framed concert photograph of an enraptured Graham clad in his trademark sailor suit ("I've just always loved boats," he says of his inspiration for the stage garb). And there are the gold records from his days with Sly: "Dance to the Music," "Everyday People," "Thank You (Falettinme Be Mice Elf Agin)," "Hot Fun in the Summertime," as well as the classic 1971 Sly album *There's a Riot Goin' On*, and Graham's solo smash from 1980, *One in a Million You*.

Surrounded by all this, the Man Who Invented Funk sits on a stool to have his picture taken. Tina excuses herself to go out in the backyard hothouse to pick fresh vegetables with the Artist's wife, Mayte, who has stopped by to gather greens to "make a salad for my honey." The CD player shuffles the three latest releases from the Artist's NPG Records label: Graham's *GCS2000*; former Rufus diva Chaka Khan's first album in six years, *Come to My House*; and a new album by the Artist, *New Power Soul*—all of which Graham says will be released early this summer.

As the booming, bass-heavy mix fills the room, *Pioneer Press* photographer John Doman sets up his equipment. Graham cradles his bass guitar. The fingers on his left hand probe the fret board absent-mindedly, while his right hand, guided by a ring finger festooned with a band that spells out *Graham* in diamonds, tickles the strings. Instinctively, Graham's wrist pivots back and forth, and his thumb (its most prominent feature: a nail so long it could belong to a supermodel or a vampire) bends back with the elasticity of a small Slinky.

He lightly slaps the instrument's top two strings.

It happens only briefly, then Graham goes back to the business of posing. But it is a moment loaded with musical history, and so intimate: it is the equivalent of Bo Diddley giving a private lesson on the Bo Diddley beat, or having Elvis Presley explain, one on one, how he came up with his hip swivel. Graham calls it "thumpin' and pluckin'," but the most widely used term for what he does is *slap bass*. It is a style familiar to every post-Vietnam musician who has ever picked up an electric bass guitar. It has influenced countless players, including Kool and the Gang, Bootsy Collins, and Prince, and has been sampled by a legion of hip-hop acts over the past two decades. And the man who came up with it never wanted to.

"I was a guitar player!" says Graham. "When I was fifteen, my mother, who played piano and sang, and I started playing clubs together. I was playing guitar, and we had a drummer. Then the drummer left, and I went out and rented a St. George bass.

"So it was just piano and bass. And to make up for not having the bass drum, I would thump the strings with my thumb. To make up for not having that backbeat, I'd pluck the strings with my fingers. Not thinking I was creating some new style, I was; I was just trying to do my job. Trying to get paid, you know? The good thing was, because I was not planning on staying with the bass, I did not care about playing 'correctly,' so to speak: the overhand, two-fingered style."

Graham was born in Beaumont, Texas, and moved to Oakland, Calif., when he was three years old. He started his career as a dancer, and played drums, clarinet, and saxophone in his high school band. He made his first record when he was thirteen with his band, the Five Riffs. In the mid-'60s, he hooked up with Sly Stone (née Sylvester Stewart), a disc jockey and producer in the Bay Area. In the late '60s and early '70s, Sly & the Family Stone served as a pop Petri dish that wed psychedelia with rock, gave birth to funk, and celebrated peace, love, black, white, and togetherness.

"Our first record was okay, but our second, 'Dance to the Music,' was when everything started to happen," says Graham. "And because I had guitar in my heart, I wasn't afraid to experiment with things like fuzztones [guitar pedals and effects], even though they weren't making things like that for bass players yet."

Along with the group's firey live shows (their performance of "I Want to Take You Higher" at Woodstock is widely regarded as the highlight of that festival), Sly gained a reputation for being unreliable and missed twenty-six of the group's scheduled eighty gigs in 1970. Drug use was widely reported, and Graham left the band in 1972 to form Graham Central Station. The same year, he met Tina, whom he married in 1975. "She was an airline stewardess, and she used to braid everybody in the band's hair. And that takes eight hours to do! So we spent a lot of time together, and we talked about God and things," says Graham, who, at the end of the interview, gives his visitors signed copies of *Knowledge That Leads to Everlasting Life*, a Jehovah's Witness Bible-study book.

"My wife and I have been married for twenty-three years now, and I've only been away from her twice for two twenty-four-hour periods," he says. "If you see me, you see my wife and daughter. I love having my family with me, and they love me. Whenever I've traveled, I've always taken them. Even when my daughter was tiny, she was at all the recording sessions. I mean, my wife was breastfeeding and singing backup vocals. That's just the way it is. It's a blessing. Families should be together as much as they can."

The Grahams spent the past seven years in Jamaica, from where Larry worked as a session player and/or toured with the likes of the Crusaders, Carlos Santana, Aretha Franklin, Stanley Clarke, and Stanley Jordan. Last year, the Artist (whom Graham met once in 1975 when both musicians were recording for Warner Bros.) recruited Larry for one of his legendary postconcert jams in Nashville. That night led to Graham Central Station opening for several of the Artist's Jam of the Year tour dates, and to the Grahams' relocation to Chanhassen.

Ever since his "Purple Rain" days, Prince has tried to give back to his childhood heroes. He resuscitated George Clinton's career, attempted to do the same with Mavis Staples, and has now forged a similar mutual admiration society with Graham and Khan. The trio performed at the recent taping of the Essence Awards '98, which will be broadcast May 21 on the Fox network (WFTC-TV, Channel 29).

Until then, funk fans can catch the Man Who Invented Funk Friday nights–Saturday mornings at Paisley Park, where Graham Central Station and the New Power Generation have been holding regular late-night jams that often go until sun up. But like funk itself, the scheduling of such gigs is all about feeling. "It's an interchange between hearts," says Graham. "We love what we do, and we love to share it. And it just happens. Like right now, I don't know if we're going to play this Friday or not. I don't know if anybody knows. I don't know if it matters."

These days, Chanhassen is home to several companies, including one whose marquee on Highway 5 reads, "Experience is a guide post, not a hitching post." It could be the philosophy of a motivational seminar innoculated businessperson, or a still-hungry founding father of funk. Back at his new home, as Graham hugs his visitors good-bye and raves about his wonderful, friendly neighbors in Minnesota, the voice coming out of the stereo speakers is also his. Over an unmistakable, prototypical slapping bass line, it sings, "I don't wanna be worshipped, I don't wanna be no star. I just wanna play funky music, I just wanna play guitar." ∎

Those Midnight Treks Are Worth a Princely Sum

June 5

TONIGHT, SOMETIME BETWEEN MIDNIGHT AND 2, WHILE the rest of the Twin Cities is tucked away in bed and the denizens of clubland are winding down, P. D. Larson will kiss his wife good night. He'll grab a Coke from the refrigerator and some cassette tapes from his music collection, perch himself by a window in his Northeast Minneapolis home, and wait for his friend Kevin Schwartz to pick him up.

When Schwartz arrives, Larson will hop in the car, and the two friends will briefly talk about their workdays: Schwartz at the Minnesota Department of Transportation, Larson at his dad's liquor warehouse. They'll discuss music, mostly, and listen to tapes or Art Bell. As they head out Highway 5 toward Paisley Park Studios in Chanhassen, a sort of caffeine rush will wake them up, and an air of anticipation will fill the car. "It's exactly twenty-seven minutes to get out there. Believe me, I know," says Larson. "I can tell you exactly what spot on the highway I'll be at in fifteen minutes, and twenty. I know this thing like the back of my hand."

Since February 7 at Paisley, the Artist Formerly Known as Prince has performed a free, open-to-anyone concert virtually every Friday night/Saturday morning, and Larson and Schwartz are among the few hardy souls who have attended almost every one. Of course, there's no guarantee that the Artist, who celebrates his fortieth birthday Sunday, will perform tonight. But given the string of great shows they've seen over the past three months, Larson and Schwartz plan to make the trek. "My guiding principle at these shows is: you miss 'em at your own risk," says Larson, a forty-two-year-old self-professed "retired rock critic" and music fanatic who covered Prince for various publications in the '70s and '80s. "That doesn't mean you can see every one, but I think it's something of a golden opportunity."

"When you think about it, it's pretty unprecedented that a major rock star would invite people over every Friday night for free chips, pop, and a concert," says Schwartz, twenty-nine. "I don't think it's ever been done before."

Of late, the Paisley drill has been this: a handful of diehards start lining up at the back door of the studio's smallish annex at around 12:30 a.m and wait until bouncers open the doors between 1:00 and 1:45 A.M. The Artist and some version of the New Power Generation, who are often joined by former Sly & the Family Stone and Graham Central Station bassist Larry Graham, hit the stage anytime between 2 and 4 A.M. "You usually get inside at around 2, then it's a total crapshoot," says Larson. "It could start within fifteen, twenty minutes, or an hour. The worst case we saw was when it started at 4:40, and he played until 6:10. We walked out and the birds were chirping and the sun was up."

Most mornings, the proceedings feel more like an intimate party than a concert. A single blue light bathes the stage, and the sound system is often overpoweringly muddy. More often than not lately, the crowds have consisted of three hundred people or less. No show has lasted less than ninety minutes, and each one has been completely different from the last: there have been experimental jams with new material ("Mad Sex," "Back in My Arms Again"), covers (Joni Mitchell's "Case of You," Elvis Presley's "Teddy Bear," Sly & the Family Stone medleys) and obscure Prince/Artist songs ("Bambi," "Bustin' Loose") and classics ("Sign o' the Times," "Kiss," "Sexy MF," "If I Was Your Girlfriend," "Days of Wild," "1999," "She's Always in My Hair," "Erotic City").

That's what has kept Larson and Schwartz staying up late at Paisley—at a time when many of the Artist's most loyal fans wouldn't walk across the street to see him. Earlier this year, the Artist sold preorders of his *Crystal Ball* four-CD set to fans via his 1-800-NEW-FUNK number, though now the Internet is awash in grousings from former fans who haven't received them. For many, the last straw was when the Artist's lawyers sent out cease-and-desist letters to fans who were operating unauthorized websites.

But such beefs are easy to forgive, if not forget, when you're up close and personal with the musician who is widely regarded as the greatest live performer of his generation. "If they were crappy shows, or even just mediocre shows, it wouldn't be that big of a deal: so what? You've got access to the guy," says Larson, who still hasn't received his preordered copy of *Crystal Ball*. "But the fact is, every show in this residency has had at least one moment where you're watching it, and you're just thinking to yourself, 'This is insane.' There's an air of unrealness about it, because you're watching this incredible performer doing these incredible shows—almost without exception—and essentially, there's no one there, and it's getting next to no press. I've even told people who were supposedly into music, and they go [indifferently], 'Oh. Prince played last night? Really?' It almost feels like a fantasy."

To be sure, many of their friends may believe Larson and Schwartz to have a couple of purple screws loose, though not the kindred spirits who have made Paisley pilgrimages from Toronto, San Francisco, Des Moines, Kansas City, Milwaukee, and points between. They all get their information from an underground e-mailing that announces the shows late Fridays. But recently, that information has proven unreliable, and as a result Larson and Schwartz missed a show last month that was, by all reports, one of the best. They're still kicking themselves for that one, and now the two friends embark on their twenty-seven-minute drive every Friday, with or without any prior information on, as Larson calls it, "a hope and a prayer."

Which aptly describes tonight's status. Schwartz points out

that the Artist played concerts this week—in Indianapolis and Montgomery, Alabama—and that the former Prince and the New Power Generation are scheduled to be the lone guests on *Vibe* Monday (12:05 A.M., Channel 9). All that activity leads Schwartz to speculate that the Artist will take a break from performing tonight. Then again . . .

"I'll probably go out there, even if I don't hear anything, just to sort of pay my dues," says Larson, laughing. "I'll drive all the way out there and see the locked gate. It is weird. I find it unusually hard to explain to people who say they're music fans, because you get looks: 'Oh, you go out there at 2:30 in the morning, do you? Where? Out in Chanhassen? Hmmm.' But of all my rock fan experiences, it's been the biggest, most intense rush I've had. You certainly don't go out there to be cool, or to hang, or to be seen. I go out there because of the music, pure and simple. You're seeing something that's special. It's not like an arena show; it's not even like a club show. It's like going to a rehearsal, or a jam session, or a studio session, and sitting behind the glass and watching." ■

TAFKAP Offers Up Sweet Jam at Free A.M. Funk-Fest

November 28

A WEEK AGO FRIDAY NIGHT/SATURDAY MORNING, NEW York City got a taste of a ritual that has become familiar to anyone who has ventured out to Paisley Park over the past two months. This past Friday night/Saturday morning, it was back to the home turf for the Artist Formerly Known as Prince as he and his band, the New Power Generation, delivered a two-hour concert that was equal parts experimental jam and greatest hits revue. On April 11, the Artist took the Irving Plaza stage in Manhattan at 3 A.M. with two of his childhood heroes, ex-Rufus singer Chaka Khan and ex–Sly & the Family Stone and Graham Central Station bassist Larry Graham.

Many of the attendees were said to have grumbled about the late start that night, but around these parts Paisley regulars have come to know the drill: power-nap during the day on Friday, or start hitting the java around 1 A.M. on Saturday. In New York, in front of a crowd that included actors Wesley Snipes, Chris Rock, and Rosie Perez, and musicians Billy Corgan, Mariah Carey, Vernon Reid, and Joan Osborne, the Artist played sideman, as the concert reportedly turned into an old-school funk variety show that reintroduced the Big Apple to two of soul music's most legendary names. The set that night (which for anyone who wasn't on the guest list cost $75 a head) consisted mostly of Rufus and Sly songs and featured cameos by George Benson and Doug E. Fresh.

But Saturday morning, 150 hard-core fans paid nothing to hear the Artist play his own songs. A small cardboard collection box for the Artist's Love 4 One Another charity was set up at Paisley's entrance, and at one point he playfully admonished the crowd for the mostly empty box. "Wassup with that?" he said. "This is free funk!"

What a bargain. The entire performance was delivered without stage lights, which gave the proceedings a smoky but never sleepy vibe. The set, which presumably acted as a warm-up for upcoming shows this week in Washington, D.C., Philadelphia, and Chicago, kicked off with a meandering rockabilly-jazz version of Elvis Presley's "Teddy Bear," which was followed by a supremely nasty and expletive-filled extended version of "Days of Wild," one of the highlights of the Artist's latest three-CD set *Crystal Ball*. From there, the band snaked its way through a loose, casual array of songs, with the Artist bouncing from guitar to bass to drums to synthesizer and singing/rapping songs like "18 and Over," "She's Always in My Hair," "Kiss," and a grand finale of "1999."

Two years ago, Oprah Winfrey asked the Artist what he most wanted people to know about him. His mouth contorted into that goofy corkscrew grin of his, then he answered: "The music." And that, beyond everything else that his fans have been griping about of late—be it business dealings, cease-and-desistings, or religious leanings—is what always rises to the top.

Indeed, what will be remembered about Saturday morning will be this snapshot: a phenomenal musician boxing his way out of the trappings of legend, standing on top of a speaker bank in front of a crowd smaller than most warm-up bands at O'Gara's Garage draw, thumping his bass like he was playing Shea Stadium, putting out like he had something to prove, then getting back down on stage to snap towels, surf the funk, and putter with some new toys on his keyboard, like he was screwing around in practice. At Paisley, there were no stars in the house, but the Artist rocked it hard, like he was playing for the first, or last, time. At the end of such performances, it's customary for musicians to tell their faithful, "Good night!" But with the clock nearing 5 A.M. and birds outside chirping a faint, annoying wake-up call, the Artist said, "Good morning!" and left the stage. Until next time. ∎

It's Party Time

"1999" Is More Than Just a Date. The Former Prince's Millennial Anthem Is Heading Back to Herald the Dawn of a New Age

December 6

FEEL IT? HERE IT COMES. RUMBLING THROUGH THE POP culture zeitgeist like a supernova, a storm cloud of sound gathering as much momentum as it is dust. Those new-wave synthesizers. Those drums that sound like Pong. That automaton voice, promising, "Don't worry. I. Won't. Hurt you. I. Only. Want you. To have some fun." It's . . .

Do we have to say it?

"1999." Not the year, nor the album. The song. Soon, very soon—weeks, days, then mere minutes 'til midnight, and on into the new millennium—the 1982 hit penned by the artist then known as Prince will be everywhere. Deejays at radio stations and clubs all over the globe are readying their CD decks, searching for that perfect New Year's Eve remix that will convey the precise medley of irony, joy, and dread that the moment demands. Irony, because (duh) that's the tenor of the times. Joy, because at its core, the song is a monster of funky celebration. And dread, because the sound everyone will be dancing to is, and was, partially the sound of fear and loathing.

Just ask Bobby Z (nee Bobby Rivkin), former drummer for Prince and the Revolution, who helped record and played countless renditions of "1999" during the *1999* and *Purple Rain* tours from 1982 to 1985:

> During one of the early tours, we checked into a hotel, and they had HBO, which was a pretty big deal. Nobody had cable yet. And on HBO was that Orson Welles show on Nostradamus. It was about 1999, and all his predictions. I don't know if that was a direct influence [on the song)], but I know that we all saw it, and we were talking about the end of the world and getting all freaked out.
>
> And Prince's theory was we better hurry up and make it huge, because the world's gonna end. So we took a sort of doomsday approach. We were all young and scared that we were going to get blown up by nuclear bombs. And I think it's still a fear. We were always talking about it, and I think if you look at his website now [www.love4oneanother.com], he's always prophesying—and, probably, rightly so. I mean, there's greed, and money, and people selling nuclear warheads like they're potato chips.

Prince's fifth album, *1999*, was released in 1982, on the heels of the previous year's *Controversy*. At the time, Prince was still a rising star. *Dirty Mind* and *Controversy* had attracted critical praise and a cult following, but mainstream success had eluded him.

The title track was the album's first single, and though it gleaned plenty of airplay on black radio, it stiffed on pop radio. That much was true until the album's second single, "Little Red Corvette," crossed over to pop radio and became Prince's first smash hit. (It was along with Michael Jackson's "Beat It" the same year the first videos by black artists to break MTV's color barrier.) After the success of "Corvette," Prince's label, Warner Bros. Records, re-released "1999" as a single. It peaked at No. 9 and spent two years on the pop charts.

"*1999* was the album that signaled Prince's arrival, so to speak," says Alan Leeds, who signed on as Prince's tour manager midway through the *1999* tour in 1982. "*Purple Rain* was the gorilla, but *1999* opened the door. What it means to me now is that I think that in writing the song, he—and certainly I, in listening to the song—underestimated how quick seventeen years go by. Because at the time, 1999 seemed like this esoteric benchmark of a generation, and the millennium seemed like [a million years away]. Back then, 1999 felt like a time when we'd have condos on the moon."

"Back then" was 1982, the year of *Dallas, Dynasty, Three's Company, E.T., the Extra-Terrestrial, Gandhi, Sophie's Choice,* John Mellencamp, Toto, and Olivia Newton-John. The streets of America were infested with a new drug called crack, and hospitals were struggling with a new disease called AIDS. Genital herpes reached epidemic proportions, the Falkland Islands war was raging, and Ronald Reagan, talking about the Peacemaker MX missile, said, "Our children should not grow up frightened. They should not fear the future."

That was the environment that hatched "1999"—though hardly from a doom-and-gloom perspective. "I think it means to enjoy life, and live life to your fullest, even though it's possible that the prophecies of the Bible may come true, and the world may end someday, and a resurrection takes place," says keyboardist Matt Fink (aka Dr. Fink), who toured and recorded extensively with Prince and the Revolution. "Being a Jewish boy, it's hard for me to relate to that thing, but Prince is into that, and we got an education about it when we were out there [on the road] with him."

Along with the rest of the *1999* album, the title track was recorded in the twenty-four-track basement studio of Prince's old purple house in Chanhassen, which came to be known as "Uptown." The Revolution—keyboardists Fink and Lisa Coleman, guitarist Dez Dickerson, bassist Mark Brown and drummer Rivkin (Jill Jones, a poet/musician and Prince protégée from Ohio, sang some backup and appears in the "1999" video as a visual foil to Coleman)—played bit parts, since Prince recorded most of the music himself.

The only recent public comment the former Prince has made about 1999 came in October, when *BET Tonight* host Tavis Smiley asked the Artist if he had any thoughts on the song or the year. "Yes," said the former Prince, clasping his hands, a mischievous grin arching his eyebrows. "If the sky has blood in it, blue and red make purple." Cryptic as usual but, really, what else can he say? He doesn't need to explain it or play it because it's already in the ether.

When you say "1999," your subconscious sings the song ("Don't you wanna go?"), because we've all been singing it for so long. For almost two decades, it has been a convenient fallback for headline writers, party invitations, etc. Now how does the writer of such a song compete with—pay tribute to—that?

A more interesting question is, did he know? Seventeen years ago, when he was recording it, did Prince realize that he was putting something down for the ages? Something that would become an omnipresent anthem that, for one night anyway, will most likely displace "Auld Lang Syne" at any party worth its salt? "I wouldn't put anything past him," says Rivkin.

At the end of 1998, rumors about "1999" have been flying. Michael Jackson reportedly approached the former Prince about doing a duet of the song. The Artist has reportedly recorded his own version to undermine any promotional gambits by Warners, which has reissued the single to radio stations and slapped stickers on Prince's double-CD set, *The Hits/The B-Sides*, that reads, "Contains the original version of '1999.'"

Perhaps the surest sign of the song's forthcoming dominance occurs in the form of a curio unique to the '90s—backlash on a website. At "We Don't Want to Party Like It's 1999!" (www.ournamehere.com/no1999) organizers offer "No 1999!" T-shirts and suggest boycotts of radio stations that play the song. Still, Warner Bros. is entertaining offers and proposals from advertising agencies that want to secure rights to the song to hawk everything from beer to underwear. "A lot of things have been tossed about, but nothing definitive has been closed yet," Les Bider, chairman of Warner Chappell Music, the publishing firm that controls the rights to the song, told the *Los Angeles Times*. "The thing is, any advertiser who wants to link this to a project would have to demand exclusivity, and that comes with a huge premium."

What that means for Prince is huge exposure and huge royalties (an estimated 85 percent of all income from the song will go to Warners, and 15 percent to the Artist) that go far beyond anything that the then-twenty-three-year-old Prince could have imagined when he penned the opening words, "I was dreaming when I wrote this, forgive me if it goes astray."

Then again, maybe that's not the point. Maybe money doesn't matter tonight. The former Prince is scheduled to tour Europe through most of December, and he'll reportedly be in either Egypt or Spain on New Year's Eve. Clearly, he doesn't seem interested in looking back, or capitalizing on a situation that most performers, in this decade of the dollar, wouldn't think twice about cashing in on. "If I was his manager and my job was to make him money, it would be easy," laughs Leeds. "It would be pay-per-view, the concert of all concerts, and I would have made him stay off the road all year and built up to this megamillion-dollar thing. It would have been satellite [broadcast], all over the world, from Mount McKinley or something ludicrous that nobody's done before, and, 'Here it is!' But that's so cheesy, and so obvious. And if, in fact, that's what he's thinking, hats off."

What the Critics Said about *1999* (the Album)

Like every black pop auteur, Prince commands his own personal groove, and by stretching his flat funk forcebeat onto two discs' worth of deeply useful dance tracks he makes his most convincing political statement to date—about race, the one subject where his instincts always serve him reliably. I mean, you don't hang on his every word regarding sex or the end of the world, now do you? (A−)

—ROBERT CHRISTGAU, *Village Voice*

The largely dance-oriented *1999* is his first real tour-de-force. Prince exercises even greater skill than before, and when he couples that with some restraint, the results are incredibly gratifying. (The first side alone has three of his best-ever cuts: "1999," "Little Red Corvette" and "Delirious.") Gratuitous sexuality and stylistic indulgences that overstretch tracks make the double-album set less than an unmitigated success; all the same, sometimes his talent is so dazzling that you don't notice (or care about) his excesses.

—JIM GREEN, *The Trouser Press Record Guide*

The padding on this two-record set is nowhere near as distracting—or boring—as it was on *Controversy*, while the melodies are stronger and the lyrics are much more pointed.

In other words, Prince has returned to the tense, exciting battleground of sexual politics he temporarily deserted after

1980's *Dirty Mind*. Once again, it is not straining the truth to use the words "Prince" and "greatness" in the same sentence. (9 out of possible 10)

—RICK SHEFCHIK, *St. Paul Dispatch*, November 1982

[*1999*] is pornographic pandering. This intractable little guy needs a collaborator, a trusting friend, or just a little whisper from his Friend above to control his genius.

—JON BREAM, *Minneapolis Tribune*, November 1982

Neither naively optimistic nor gloomily nihilistic, *1999* was a brilliantly eyes-wide-open affair. It said, yes, we are in fact hurtling toward oblivion, let me show you how to enjoy the ride.

—MARY ELIZABETH WILLIAMS, *Salon*

This double-album mingling of politics and sex features Prince's sturdiest dance grooves and his first crossover hits ("Little Red Corvette," "Delirious" and the title track). This album is a near-masterpiece.

—JOHN FLOYD, *All Music Guide to Rock*

The plain fact is that much of *1999* sounds disappointingly familiar. Perhaps plagiarists like the Time and Vanity 6 have forced his hand, perhaps the danger of self-parody called for a dramatic shift of emphasis, but, whatever the motivation, *1999* sounds like a collection of crudely calculated maneuvers toward popular ingratiation.

—STEVE SUTHERLAND, *Melody Maker*, November 1982 ■

Artist, Mayte Call It Quits . . . in a Way, for Now

Symbolic Remarriage May Follow Annulment

December 15

T HE ARTIST FORMERLY KNOWN AS PRINCE AND HIS WIFE of almost three years, Mayte Garcia-Nelson, are getting divorced. Sort of.

And remarried. Sort of.

The Chanhassen-based musical maverick held a press conference Friday in Madrid, Spain, to announce that he and Mayte will annul their marriage and be rejoined in a "symbolic" ceremony on Valentine's Day 1999. "My wife and I want to end our marriage, to proceed without any sort of contract held by social conventions, and to strengthen our union with an individual proceeding, purely spiritual," the former Prince read from a prepared statement, reprinted in Madrid's daily *El Mundo* newspaper Saturday. "We will return [to Spain] on February 14 to be united in a symbolic manner, leaving aside legal proceedings that do no more than separate people. Mayte and I are joined for life, and the best way to demonstrate it is to do away with the legal bonds that people demand."

Of course, this isn't the first time the former Prince has bucked man-made contracts. His much-ballyhooed clash with his former record company, Warner Bros. Records, was all about a contract he signed. Since fulfilling it last year, he now records for his own label, NPG Records, which he says doesn't do contracts.

The former Prince and Mayte, who bought a home in Marbella, Spain, earlier this year, were married on Valentine's Day 1996 at Park Avenue United Methodist Church in South Minneapolis. In Madrid on Friday, the musician told reporters that contracts "are made by man to guarantee the possibility of divorce," and "conventional marriage ceremonies are totally counter to our beliefs."

The former Prince and his band, the New Power Generation, are currently on tour in Spain. According to Madrid's *ABC* newspaper, a small incident took place at the press conference when a local musician presented the former Prince with a zambomba as "a Christmas instrument." The ex-Prince asked the musician to explain the concept of Christmas to him "because I don't understand what Christmas means. It seems to be a ridiculous convention that everyone assumes."

In related ex-Prince news, cable TV's VH1 is scheduled to air an interview with the Artist conducted by Spice Girl Mel B (aka Scary Spice), Wednesday at 8 P.M. Also, he is preparing to release a new recording of his 1982 hit "1999." The CD will feature seven remixes of the song (including dance, rap, and reggae) and can be seen as a direct retaliation to the pending (and expected) newfound popularity of the original version, re-released by Warners. "The new record is different from the Warner Bros. edition in several ways," the former Prince told reporters in Spain. "But the fundamental difference is that on this occasion, 100 percent of the income will go to the author—me. [With the original recording] Warner takes 85 percent of the money, and I only get 15 percent. I am not telling people not to buy the Warner version. Simply they should compare and choose the one they like best. And yes, the new version was made with the latest technology and sounds much better. Also, it is better because the recording reflects my relationship with Mayte." ■

1999

Santana, Two Hot Guests Make Some Music Magic

June 21

THE NORTHROP AUDITORIUM STAGE HAS PLAYED HOST TO numerous dignitaries, college graduations, and other historic happenings over the years. But Sunday at exactly 10:10 p.m, the sold-out hall bore witness to one of its all-time most memorable musical moments. At the halfway point of Santana's two-hour-and-fifteen-minute performance, guitar icon Carlos Santana invited two Twin Cities residents up onstage: Larry Graham and the Artist Formerly Known as Prince. The two musicians strapped on their bass and guitar, respectively, and launched into a nasty, ad-libbed funk-fusion number (whose chorus-chant went "One Love"). In the context of the concert, the ten-minute jam didn't stand out especially as a musical highlight, but when you stepped back for a moment to consider just what was happening onstage, it was nothing short of extraordinary.

There was Santana, the man who has been credited with launching Latin rock in the late '60s and one of rock's most influential guitarists, firing off leads with the former Prince, the man who brought a nation's libido to its knees in the '80s and who remains one of the few true musical iconoclasts of the '90s, bumping off the slap bass of Graham, the man who acted as the midwife, if not inventor, of funk in the early '70s with Sly & the Family Stone.

Time warp, baby.

With the scent of incense and pot in the air, and the psychedelic light show behind the stage, there was a vibe to the proceedings that beamed everybody in the room back to the era when Sara Jane Olson was just another revolutionary named

Kathleen Soliah. Still, the concert was hardly a relic for the Rock 'n' Roll Hall of Fame. Santana kicked off with a liquid soul jam, fueled by the horn section from Ozomatli, the Los Angeles world music group that opened the show. From there, the big band (a keyboard player, two drummers, one bassist, three percussionists, one forgettable singer, and one forgettable rapper) indulged in jam band grooves, Caribbean-flavored rhythms, and Santana's taut, dramatic, playful, orchestral, expressive, and often glorious leads.

Most of the songs, which relied on competing crescendos and call-and-response improvisation, were the stuff that other bands use as encores. Songs included "Black Magic Woman," Marvin Gaye's "I Want You," and Tito Puente's "Oye Como Va" (which the former Prince and Graham have been covering at their late-night Paisley Park jams recently). But frankly, the material was a distant second to Santana's flash-but-not-flashy musicianship. His fingers flew across the fretboard with such vigor that there was a sense that his playing comes from somewhere deep inside, not years of practice.

For the first encore, the three percussionists jammed so hard it sent an ominous mechanical noise blaring through Northrop. "We're smokin'," said one player. "We just set off the fire alarm." He wasn't kidding, which only added to the historical weirdness of a night that saw three giants walk with each other, and among us. My question is: anybody get any pictures? ■

Symbolic Agreement Reached

Prince Drops *Uptown* Suit. Fan Magazine
Will Not Use Symbol, List Bootlegs

July 30

THE ARTIST FORMERLY KNOWN AS PRINCE HAS DROPPED HIS lawsuit against *Uptown* magazine, a nonprofit fan-written and -produced publication, which he sued in February. Among other things, the Artist was hoping to slap *Uptown* with a cease-and-desist order similar to the ones he issued to various fan-generated websites earlier this year. According to a statement issued by *Uptown*'s lawyers Thursday, the Artist has entered into an agreement with *Uptown* that says, among other items, that the magazine will no longer publish discographies of bootleg Prince recordings. The agreement guarantees *Uptown*'s First Amendment rights, and the right to freely comment on the Artist's music—unreleased and released—as it has since it first launched as a fanzine in Sweden in 1991.

The Artist also wanted *Uptown* to stop using the unpronounceable symbol that the Chanhassen-based musician adopted in 1993, which *Uptown* had been using "out of respect." *Uptown* editors have already stopped using the symbol—the software font for which the Artist provided them—and have no plans to call the musician anything but his given name. "We were pleased to achieve a resolution of the case that upheld the right of a publisher to comment freely through a magazine and website," said David Evans, of the Boston law firm Hanify & King, one of two firms that represented *Uptown*, in the statement. ∎

Formerly Prince's

His Stuff Brings in the Fans. The Artist Has
Garage Sale at Studio

August 15

THERE WAS A GARAGE SALE IN CHANHASSEN ON SATUR-
day. But instead of balloon-festooned cardboard signs
trumpeting the address, customers were greeted with placards
that read "CASH ONLY. No bags allowed inside. No photos allowed. No cameras allowed."

Clearly, this was not your Auntie Molly's garage sale.

When the Artist Formerly Known as Prince's website (www
.love4oneanother.com) announced earlier this week that he
was holding a garage sale at Paisley Park Studios this weekend, an image of Minnesota's funkiest son bartering over old
dishes and well-thumbed paperbacks sprang to mind. The Artist was nowhere to be found at Paisley Saturday afternoon, but
hundreds of his fans were. They stood in line for more than an
hour to scarf up memorabilia, displayed on tables inside Paisley's cavernous indoor soundstage. The sale continues today
from noon to 6 P.M.

Besides tour merchandise, most priced at less than $10,
there were bigger items including keyboards ($100–$200),
tambourines emblazoned with the Artist symbol ($50), and
equipment cases stenciled with "PRN Productions" ($75). "I
got a really sweet barber chair for fifty bucks," said Dave Wolf,
singer/guitarist for local rockers the Vibro Champs.

As of 1 P.M., many of the large items already were adorned
with sold stickers, including a pair of mahogany leather chairs,
a Victorian dining room set, and two neon signs from the *Sign
o' the Times* tour, which read "Coin Castle" and "All Nude." Many
fans coveted a yellow neon symbol sign displayed in a wooden
crate but were deterred by the $200 price. "My Prince symbol
necklace got stolen two years ago, and I've been looking for

one ever since," said Lars Larson, twenty, of Robbinsdale who stood in line clutching his new necklace, two posters, and a bottle of Get Wild perfume. Larson and other enthusiasts had nowhere to turn for Artist/Prince merchandise since Paisley's mail order line has proved dicey and the New Power Generation store closed in 1996.

Some might point to the sale as another sign that the former Prince is in financial trouble, but Paisley sources insist that the soundstage was turning into a cluttered storage space. Brett Dahlof, twenty-one, of Bloomington had another thought: "He's always doing stuff for the fans. He does concerts out here every weekend—for seven dollars or free. I think he just likes to give back to the fans." Tom Branham, fifty, of Edina was hoping for an even bigger favor. "I've been out here for shows before," he said. "They're incredible. And because of his reputation for doing off-the-wall things, I was harboring a secret hope that he would play today."

Some fans were buying birthday presents and stocking stuffers. Patty Dean of the Minnesota Historical Society bought some fanzines and a Joffrey Ballet Billboards poster for the Historical Society's pop music collection.

Others were puzzled by the notion of a garage sale. "If you came here with, like, a thousand bucks, bought all this stuff, and didn't have any attachment to it, you could put it on ebay. Right away you'd make a killing," Wolf said. "Yeah, but that's not what this is about," said Wolf's friend, Kii Arens, of the local band Flipp, who bought two neon signs. "A garage sale is like, 'C'mon over and hang out.' But I don't see any hot dogs or pop or homemade cookies. I'm kinda bummed out about that." ■

Purple Pride
The Artist's Ten Best Local Gigs

<u>September 3</u>

D OWNTOWN MINNEAPOLIS. NINETEEN-NINETY-NINE. "1999." Labor Day. The hardest-working man in show business. If that's not a recipe for history, I don't know what is.

And if you still have doubts that the little guy won't deliver a write-it-down-for-the-ages performance at Monday's Mill City Music Festival finale, consider that the Artist Formerly Known as Prince—as competitive a player onstage as Michael Jordan was on the court—is not about to be upstaged by his old cronies Alexander O'Neal, the Time, or even his mentor, Larry Graham and Graham Central Station. But before we fast-forward to Monday's performance, it's worth remembering how he, and we, got here. Here's one man's fond look back at the ten most memorable local live gigs ever thrown down by Prince/the Artist:

1. December 9–10, 1997, Target Center and Paisley Park. A ridiculously energetic two-and-a-half-hour arena stop on the Jam of the Year tour, followed by two sets (eighty minutes and forty minutes) at an even more energetic open jam between the New Power Generation and Graham Central Station at Paisley. When I got home that morning at 6 A.M., I wrote a column for the next day, calling it "probably the most amazing night of music I have ever witnessed." Twenty-one months later, I'd like to scratch the "probably."

The *Chicago Tribune*'s Greg Kot recently put the Artist at No. 2 (behind the Jesus Lizard) on his list of the top ten greatest live performers of the '90s. You read that right—"the '90s." While most of his live legend was made with the majority in the '80s, the minority who have continued to pay attention to the Artist in the '90s have done so largely because of his stripped-down guitar pyrotechnics and funk-fueled rapture. All of which were set on "superhuman" this night/morning.

2. March 8, 1982, First Avenue. For many, the several unannounced sets that Prince and his bands performed at First Avenue in the '80s are the club shows against which all club shows will forever be measured. This was the zenith. The night after the *Controversy* tour played to seven thousand at Met Center, Prince (or "Rude Boy," as his ska lingo-pilfering T-shirts of the day read) and his band, clad in black, cut loose with elongated funk and jazz workouts that lasted well past 1 A.M.

3. March 9, 1981, Sam's (later First Avenue). My first time and his maiden voyage at the club he'd help make famous. In the middle of a lackluster show by Joe "King" Carrasco at Duffy's, I realized I'd made the wrong gig choice and flew over to Sam's. Prince was tearing it up at his fourth solo appearance in town. It was the dawn of *Dirty Mind*, and I was blown away by this impudent new cat's trench coat, leggings and G-string, and his twin Telecaster attack (with Dez Dickerson). I caught up with my brother and his new girlfriend, who were also newly spellbound. It was our first Prince show, and my brother put it into words that made the most sense to us at the time: "He's the Black Springsteen."

4. March 3, 1986, First Avenue. This post–*Purple Rain* and –*Around the World in a Day*, and pre-*Parade* and –*Sign o' the Times* greatest-hits revue caught Prince during one of his most prolific periods and at the peak of his commercial powers.

5. September 14, 1988, Met Center. The opening night of the *Lovesexy* tour found Prince at his most theatrical, with his entrance in a white '67 Thunderbird; a ménage à trois passion play among him, dancer Cat, and Sheila E.; and a stage decked out in an urban dreamscape, with a basketball hoop and swing set. I sat with Billy Bragg and the Red Stars, who were in town on their own *Workers Playtime* tour, and the sight of these Brits flipping out, as Brits are wont to do when it comes to Prince, was as hilarious as it was unforgettable.

6. May 25–26, 1994, Glam Slam and Paisley Park. It started in Glam Slam's upper deck (aka Erotic City), where the Artist had been performing intimate, mind-blowing 2 A.M. sets all week. Three hundred clubgoers were met by an exotic dancer, who led them on a scavenger hunt and ultimately to Paisley in

Chanhassen. This was in the days before the Artist was playing regular late-night jams at Paisley, so at 3 A.M., when he
said, "You like my house?" many who responded in the affir-
mative had never been there before. What I remember most
from the set are smoldering versions of "Race" and "Shhh," a
return to jaw-dropping guitar playing, and some elastic, electric blues.

7. February 13, 1994, Paisley Park. It was NBA All-Star Weekend, so there were plenty of beautiful people in the crowd of
six hundred for "The Beautiful Experience," including Will
Smith, Salt-N-Pepa, Soul Asylum, Kriss Kross, Magic Johnson, Dikembe Mutombo, David Robinson, Clyde Drexler, and
Alonzo Mourning. But the music was the most memorable aspect of this frigid night, including the debut of the gorgeous
single and video "The Most Beautiful Girl in the World" and
the most potent Artist track of the '90s, "Days of Wild."

8. December 26, 1984, St. Paul Civic Center. *Purple Rain* ma-
nia was in full effect. I'd seen a similar show at First Avenue
around the same time, with Prince atop the speakers, shooting water from his guitar during "Darling Nikki" and "Jack U
Off." But this concert—part of a five-night stand at the Civic
Center—was bigger and louder, and somehow more amazing
to see, given the hometown hoopla and the world at his feet.

9. January 12, 1992, Glam Slam. This *Diamonds and Pearls*
tour preview found Prince and band tearing it up, with a little
help from George Clinton. Most memorable snapshot: Prince
tiptoeing the length of the front bar, like a James Brown–
weaned tightrope walker.

10. October 20, 1984, 7th St. Entry. I wasn't there, but through
the wonder of bootlegs, this local legend lives on. With *Purple Rain* at the top of the film and music charts, Prince and
a few band members sauntered into the Entry and took over
the stage and the Pedal Jets' gear. A low-burn jam ensued, and
when it was over, soundman Bill Batson said, "Who was that
guy?" We may never get a full answer to that question, but a
pretty good approximation can be had whenever his funny,
funky, frisky booty is on a stage. ∎

Artist-ic License

With the Release of a New Album and a Major-
Label Alliance, the Former Prince Hopes to
Get the Bandwagon Rolling Again

November 8

DEPENDING ON WHOM YOU ASK, THE ARTIST FORMERLY
Known as Prince is (1) a musical genius, (2) a canny crafts-
man mining past glories, or (3) that kook with a glyph for a
name. But one thing no one has called the forty-one-year-old
Minneapolis native for much of this decade is (4) a hit-maker.
For a variety of reasons, the former Prince hasn't had a Top
10 single since 1994's "The Most Beautiful Girl in the World."
That lack of commercial success could come to an end Tues-
day, with the release of the Artist's new album, *Rave Un2 the
Joy Fantastic.*

The CD (produced by "Prince") features cameos by Sheryl
Crow, Ani DiFranco, Gwen Stefani from No Doubt, Chuck
D from Public Enemy, hot new Philly rapper Eve, and James
Brown saxophonist Maceo Parker. But the big news is that
the record will be released on the Artist-owned NPG Records,
through a licensing deal with Arista Records—the first time
the Artist has been affiliated with a major label since 1997's
Emancipation, which was distributed by the now-defunct EMI.
It is his first studio album for a major label since 1996's Warner
Bros.-released *Chaos and Disorder.*

"The [new] album is wonderful," said Clive Davis, Arista's
legendary founder and executive director, by phone from New
York. "It's a bristling, young, contemporary artist at the peak
of his form. When he played it for me, I was blown away. I
thought it was a major work." All of which, of course, could be
construed as record executive hoo-ha. But if *Rave*'s first single,
the stripped-down, eerily erotic, and, yes, catchy-as-all-hell

"The Greatest Romance Ever Sold," is any indication, Davis and the former Prince have a monster hit in the making.

Throughout the '90s, the absurdly prolific Artist produced several would-be hit singles. But his outlaw image with the music industry sabotaged him on the charts. Enter Davis, one of the most respected figures in the music business, the man who signed such acts as Aretha Franklin, Patti Smith, Carly Simon, Annie Lennox, and the Grateful Dead. Davis has been instrumental in resuscitating several careers, most recently that of Carlos Santana, whose record *Supernatural* (four million sold and counting) is the year's biggest surprise—to Davis, included. "The Santana situation is a wonderful shock—I can't even use the word *surprise*. I mean, you can only hope for that," he said. "It's a great album, and it's one of the most satisfying milestones of my life. But when I signed Santana, if I had done research as to why his records hadn't done better in the past twenty years, I would never have signed him. You can't do that. The music has to speak for itself."

The success of *Supernatural* very likely helped L. Londell McMillan, the former Prince's New York–based attorney, facilitate the meeting between Davis and the Artist. After freeing himself from his contract with Warner Bros., the label he signed with when he was nineteen, the Artist swore off major labels. Since then, he has established himself as one of the world's premiere independent recording artists by releasing several albums through his website (www.love4oneanother. com). All proceeds from those Internet sales go straight to the Artist—a fact he has been fond of trumpeting, in interviews and on his website.

The Arista agreement stipulates that the Artist owns his master tapes, which was a major point of contention with Warner Bros. And while his music so often refracts the joys of love and pleasure, his business muse is fueled by anger, and a distrust of the middleman. And he's not alone. "I followed his lead just on the way he makes judgment calls on how he handles his career," said Public Enemy's Chuck D, by phone from his home in New York. "The industry is a whole bunch of white executives—and I'm not talking about the color of a person's skin, I'm talking about a white mentality that says, 'N____, you can't be more than what you say you want to be. We're the power structure, and you're gonna fall in line.' We've been saying for years that there's got to be another way, and to get rid of the middleman. Public Enemy, we treat Prince like the prince that he is. He's still on the throne."

For his *Rave* part, Chuck D flew to the Twin Cities, "had a twenty-four-hour-long conversation" and recording session with the Artist at Paisley Park in Chanhassen, and flew out. Crow, who partook in a similar whirlwind session between Lilith Fair tour stops, is another one of the *Rave* collaborators who has ultimate respect for the Artist's music. But she sees his ongoing battle with the industry as being counterproductive to the artistic process. "He's really consumed with that," Crow said in an interview before her show last month at the Fine Line Music Cafe in Minneapolis. "It's difficult for me to get bogged down in that, because my life—like his—is really about making music. But I can't approach it with that kind of vehement mistrust. I feel like people are innately good, and that they just don't always do the right thing. I happen to, at this point, be in a record contract that there's nothing I can do about. So instead of spending a lot of time creating really negative juices in my body about the unfairness of my situation, I've chosen really to just concentrate on what my life's about, and that's making music."

Crow, who sings and plays harmonica on a song titled "Baby Knows," said she became a Prince fan when she heard *Dirty Mind* as a high school sophomore. That was in the '80s, after which so many fell off the purple bandwagon. But if Davis has anything to do with it, as of Tuesday the Artist will seduce them back. "He just seems very willing, and eager, with respects to this radio-friendly album, to tour and perform, and

we've gotten along great," he said. "I haven't paid much attention to his recent music or how it was distributed. To me, I was
interested in what is the music that he and I will be working
on to reach people all over the world. And that excites me tre-
mendously. He's delivered the goods, and we're more than up
to the challenge." ∎

Artist's "Rave" Less Than Fantastic, but It Ain't All Bad

November 11

EVERYTHING WE'VE COME TO KNOW AND LOVE ABOUT THE
Artist Formerly Known as Prince is all over his latest record—for better and worse.

No, this is not the groundbreaking stuff of his '80s mas-
terpieces, nor does it contain much of his best experimental
work of the '90s. But it does brim with the same scintillating
screams, melodies, and production expertise that have marked
his twenty-plus-year career. The best of the fifteen tracks are
the ballads, most notably "I Love U, but I Don't Trust U Anymore," an intimate piano-propped heartbreaker that rivals
Prince's classic "How Come U Don't Call Me Anymore?" on the
goosebump meter. "Wherever U Go, Whatever I Do" is one of
those great life lesson songs the former Prince cranks out with
astonishing regularity, while "The Sun, the Moon and Stars" is
his latest make-out-and-then-some song for the ages.

Other highpoints are the title track, built on a ghostly
Stones-by-way-of-Massive-Attack guitar riff; the sinewy sin-
gle "The Greatest Romance Ever Sold"; a funked-up version of
Sheryl Crow's "Everyday Is a Winding Road"; the raunch-rocker
"Baby Knows" (with Crow on vocals); the exuberant pop-rocker

"So Far, So Pleased" (with Gwen Stefani of No Doubt); and a hidden track, fueled by Maceo Parker's percolating saxophone.

The only real missteps are "Hot Wit You" (with Philly rapper Eve), a generic come-on that sounds as if the sexy M.F. is going through the motions of lovemaking, not to mention record making; and "Undisputed," an embarrassing declaration of hambone hubris that skewers the music industry (Stop the presses!), name-drops D'Angelo and the Roots' Questlove, and features a forgettable rap from Public Enemy's Chuck D.

In the Prince/Artist canon, *Rave Un2 the Joy Fantastic* may be a whopping commercial success but does not speak to the moment the way great music always hopes to. Nonetheless, *Rave* is a strong record, one that ultimately feels more workmanlike than inspired. ∎

Ex-Recluse Ex-Prince Is on Publicity Binge for Y2K Show

December 15

FOR THE ARTIST FORMERLY KNOWN AS PRINCE, WHO UNTIL recently has been known as the artist known as reclusive, the past couple of weeks have been something of a media blitz. Last Wednesday, the Chanhassen-based musician appeared on the *Today Show*. Friday, he was on MTV, introducing the world premiere of the video for his new single, "The Greatest Romance Ever Sold." Later Friday night, the Artist appeared on *Larry King Live* on CNN.

Incredible? Unbelievable? Get this: the former Prince has taped a segment of *The View*, which is scheduled to air Friday on ABC (10 A.M., Channel 5, in the Twin Cities). It's all to hype his pay-per-view special, *Rave Un2 the Year 2000*, which will be taped Saturday night at the Artist's Paisley Park Studios in Chanhassen and will air worldwide on New Year's Eve.

The Artist and his band, the New Power Generation, will be the concert's main attraction, along with cameo appearances by retro rocker Lenny Kravitz, gospel legend Mavis Staples, fellow Minneapolis funk pioneers The Time, and the ex-Prince's mentor, bassist Larry Graham, and members of Graham's old band, Sly & the Family Stone. An invitation-only list of what the Artist's New York press representative describes as "family and friends" will make up the audience at Saturday's taping (VH1 is auctioning off twenty pairs of tickets at www.vh1.com). The pay-per-view special (which airs at 9 P.M. local time) can be purchased through In Demand (the cable station formerly known as Viewer's Choice) for $19.99.

Of all his media appearances, the ex-Prince proved to be especially personable, funny, and wise with Larry King. The Artist talked about his career, family, spirituality, his hometown of Minneapolis, and his adopted home of Spain, where siestas allow "everybody a chance to regroup and think about life." He said he'll always have a fondness for his hometown, where he still works and plays, saying, "Minneapolis has always been the bomb. You don't have to go outside of that."

He also said he's not worried about Y2K, and that Saturday is the last time he'll perform his party-on-the-edge-of-the-apocalypse anthem, "1999." The former Prince even invited his latest best friend King to attend the taping, saying, "You need to come. It's going to be off the chart." ■

2000–2002

Open Letter to Prince: Best Gift You Can Give Is a Great New Record

June 2, 2000

D EAR PRINCE,
Have I got that right? I hear that's what they're calling you these days, because that's what you've told them to call you. Great news; people who haven't been interested in you in years are suddenly interested again. Prince is back, and all that.

Well, remember me? I'm the guy who, for the past seven years, has called you the Artist Formerly Known as Prince, the Artist, TAFKAP, and, once, Tafty. I'm the one who stuck up for you, who wrote all that glowing stuff in this newspaper and in the liner notes to your album *The Gold Experience* (I got paid exactly one dollar because I didn't want to go there with you), and now that we're on the cusp of your birthday Wednesday, and a sold-out weeklong party out at Paisley Park called Prince: A Celebration, I need to ask, What, exactly, are we celebrating?

Are we celebrating the fact that you haven't made a great record, one that the entire world cared about, in years? That your live show has turned into a stale, predictable—if phenomenally well played, as always—set of oldies and covers? That several lesser lights have made off with your crown because you've been distracted from the task at hand (making music that describes right now) by music industry–grousing, name changes, cryptic religious questions but no answers, and hype over artistry?

Count me out, even though my party invitation seems to have been lost in the mail. I'm probably on your enemies list now, because I was only moved by a few songs off your last few records (*Rave Un2 the Joy Fantastic*, *New Power Soul*, and *Crystal Ball*), and I wrote as much.

143

Then again, maybe you're not mad at me. Maybe it's just that you've moved on and you're done with me. But I'm not done with you. I care too much, and your music has meant too much to me to stop caring now. But there are plenty of people who don't care. Almost everyone I know thinks you're cooked. Don't you want to prove them wrong? Forget them—don't you want to surprise yourself? Don't you want to make one more record that nails it, that truly says something and feels innovative? Why don't you get really, truly, weird again—as weird as the times demand—and take us on another journey, not a flashback lunch?

Make no mistake: this is a challenge. I am writing to reach you. And it may be presumptuous for a lowly rock critic to attempt to tell one of the great artists of our time to wake up and smell the muse, but I happen to think that great artists are like great chefs: they've got all the skills and ingredients, but they don't know what we're hungry for if we don't tell them. And given the state of mainstream music at the moment, I am starved.

So here's the deal: for your birthday, I want a gift. I don't want an interview, or a tour of Paisley Park, or the hem of your garment. I want a great record. What you do best. Something real. Something that blows these say-nothing boy bands and bimbos, divas and playas, out of the water once and for all. And in case you haven't noticed, we could use it because these are strange days, indeed. To wit:

Last Friday, I was sitting at the Loring Bar watching a pretty cool jazz outfit, Moveable Feast, and listening to DJ Wicked spin. Three of the four people I was with admitted that they walk around this town in fear of getting shot. What is that? And why haven't we heard from you on it? Whatever happened to the guy who sang "America" and "Sign o' the Times"? Where have you gone, Prince Rogers Nelson? A nation turns its lonely eyes to you.

Why don't you call up Paul Westerberg—another Minneapolis genius your age who is going through his own struggle with silence and relevance, a guy whom I'd rather hear blow into two pop bottles on a boom box than most of the stuff that passes for "rock" these days—and do "Ebony and Ivory" for the double-oughts?

Where's your updating of "Money Don't Matter 2night?" for this cash-obsessed nation? Do you have another "Adore," the greatest love song the world doesn't know about, in you? Does another "Race" or "Uptown" percolate somewhere deep inside, something that seeks to unite the Melting Pot even as it feels like it's about to boil over? You wrote "We Gets Up" for Michael Jordan and the Chicago Bulls. How about one for Malik Sealy, and our heartbroken, wounded Wolves, that captures that specific sense of dread and fan grief that nobody's been able to express with words? How about a grand epic about this technology grog, and how it both fragments and bonds us? Or what about something small, something we can all relate to, about marriage trouble or the death of a loved one?

We are waiting, have been waiting, for your contribution. Instead, we get more funk, joy in repetition, and something called "Cybersingle." Which is fine. But heavens to Bootsy, we already know you're funky and computer savvy and cutting edge and all that. What we need are some songs that express what is in our hearts, minds, souls. Some greatness.

Maybe you're resting, or burned out, or in a fortysomething funk, waiting for the songs to come. I can relate. Been there. But you're the one who said, "Dearly beloved, we are gathered here today to get through this thing called life," and I feel like I'm going to need machetes to get through the next ten years, so it'd be nice if you had my back along the way.

And if you're afraid that your best work is behind you—and who could blame you if you did, after all the great stuff you've given the world?—remember this: when they were in their early forties, Elvis and John Coltrane were dead and Elton was coasting, but Bob Dylan made *Infidels,* Neil Young made *Freedom,* Marvin Gaye made *Here, My Dear,* Tom Waits made *Bone Machine,* Lou Reed made *New York,* John Lennon and Yoko Ono made *Double Fantasy,* Madonna made *Ray of Light,* Van Morrison made *No Guru, No Method, No Teacher,* and Miles Davis made *Bitches Brew.*

So do me a favor. Don't ignore this. When you perform at Northrop Auditorium next Tuesday, don't do an oldies show, which I already fear you're working up. Show us that you're paying attention. Seize the moment. Do you have anything left to say? If not, get out of the way. Don't tease us, because it hurts too much. And don't pretend that you care, because if you cared the way Prince used to care, you'd go into your studio and pull an all-weeker, shake yourself up, throw out the formulas that got you (us) here, splash your canvas with all the desperation, ennui, and hope of the age, and set the world on fire again.

May U live 2 see the dawn,

Jim

———

Jilted lover much? I somewhat regret writing this now. It reflects how I was feeling at the time, but knowing what I now know about writing and recording music and performing live, it's altogether arrogant and uninformed, and I recognize how difficult it is to do what Prince and ♀ did with his gifts.

The afternoon this was published, Prince summoned me out to Paisley. When I arrived, he and the band were rehearsing "When U Were Mine." When he saw me enter the soundstage, he stopped the band and said, "Are you cool for a little bit?"

I nodded yes, I was good, and they continued rehearsing for another fifteen minutes. Then he jumped offstage, said "Hey," and we started walking toward his first-floor office. As we walked down the hallway, I tried to break the ice and put my arm around him.

"You know I love you," I said.

"Security!" he yelled, and we both cracked up, but I could tell he was not happy.

When we got to his office, he said, "You can write what you want, but the kids read it and then they repeat it and believe it." (The column was already making the rounds on the nascent World Wide Web.) I apologized but also said something about the violent times we were living in and how I needed to hear from him. "The grooves are there; you just have to look 'em up," he said, and of course he was right.

I told him I was rooting for him and wondered if he wanted to have a hit record that would put him on top.

"No, no, no," he said, animatedly. "I've been to the mountaintop. There's nothing there."

Wise man.

Larry Graham joined us after a few minutes, and for the next two hours, it was just the three of us. Prince sat down and called up my column on his computer and read it back to me, line by line. When it got to the part about "the hem of your garment," he stopped and looked into my eyes.

Ahem.

"Actually," I said, "I do want the hem of your garment," and he and Graham laughed uproariously, slapping knees and Prince falling out of his chair.

Phew.

The rest of the meeting went like that, three music lovers talking about life and funk and basketball. "You got your shoes?" Prince said at one point, challenging me to a game of one-on-one. He also said, out of the blue, as new child molestation accusations swirled around Michael Jackson, "Only God and Michael know what happened, and Michael is an angel," to which Graham replied, "Amen." ∎

Spiritual, at Times Inspired,
Prince Saves Best for Last

June 15, 2000

AFTER SEVEN DAYS OF CELEBRATING HIMSELF, PRINCE
saved his best for the last forty-five minutes. The time
was 12:05 A.M. Wednesday when Prince called three of his
five former bandmates in the Revolution—keyboardist Matt
Fink, bassist Brown Mark, and drummer Bobby Z—onto the
Northrop Auditorium stage. The band roared into "America,"
and for a moment there it reminded a fellow how great Prince
was, and is.

However brief, it was the night's highlight simply because
of its sheer weirdness: four men—one ageless (Prince), one fine
(Mark), and the other two looking their age—who turned the
world on its ear in the '80s, reunited for one shaky jam. Instead
of playing it safe, or indulging in terrific-to-tedious jams, as
too much of the rest of the concert did, Prince was suddenly on
a tightrope, and it felt like anything could happen. Infused by
the power of funk and inspired by the strange chemistry, the
Revolution guys left the stage, and Prince started wildly playing the unmistakable riff to "Kiss" and teasing the crowd, saying "Thank you, good night" a few times. Then he kicked the
band into overdrive and delivered a superb rendition of one
of his most durable hits. "Kiss" was followed by a nasty reading of "Gett Off" and a lengthy jam during which the night's
fourth dance party broke out onstage with audience members
and musicians surfing the same groove.

Prince danced with a five- or six-year-old little girl, gave a
guitar to a woman in the front row (a roadie took it back at the
end of the night), and generally moved about the stage like a
funk-filled bandleader/coach. The last sight of him was dancing backstage, whipped on the beat. The concert clocked in at

three hours and forty-five minutes, with the preceding three hours serving as a study in what is both exhilarating and maddening about Prince, circa 2000.

The night opened with a video montage of highlights of Prince's career and interviews with fans who attended Prince: A Celebration. Then the man himself hit the stage, delivering eerie readings of "Anna Stesia" (during which he said, "We're here to celebrate life—without God, there is no life," then asked the crowd to sing "Love is God, God is love") and "The Greatest Romance Ever Sold" (during which he sang about "the greatest man who ever lived. . . . If you don't believe in Jesus Christ, I got nuthin' to say to ya"). Then it quickly turned into a cheesy sampling of greatest hits.

Though the old material was expertly played, even Prince seemed bored with it, barely breaking a sweat. Thankfully, the rest of the show turned into a sprawling jam, much like Prince's late-night sessions at Paisley Park. "Pretty Man" became a pretty jam with saxophone giant Maceo Parker wailing, rapper Q-Tip rhyming, and Prince playing guitar, drums, and bass keyboard. With a billowing fireball on the video screen above, and bassist Larry Graham and Prince both playing bass guitars, the band cast out a dark, dirty (if G-rated) version of the Prince freedom anthem "Days of Wild." Gospel singer Angie Stone got up onstage for a few tunes, including the crowd-pleaser "Dr. Feelgood." And though the set reverted to retro mode with bassist Larry Graham singing Sly & the Family Stone's "Everyday People" and Prince doing Hooked-on-Prince versions of "Raspberry Beret" and "Take Me with U," it also included plaintive renditions of "Nothing Compares 2 U" and "Adore."

Those were the moments that felt real, and even, sometimes, really daring. In that sense, I even dug it when Prince questioned my faith in God and called me a "fool" from the stage for writing a critical column about him recently. Not because he has any insight into me, but because it showed a sense of urgency, of anger, of being in the moment, instead of an indulgence in star power, showmanship, and fuzzy nostalgia.

Still, too often Tuesday night, especially when he was splicing and dicing his old hits into medleys, one got the sense of what it must have been like to see Michael Jordan play baseball: you know there's a great artist, a true pioneer in there somewhere, but his uniform doesn't quite fit. That's the bad news. The good news is that the last time Prince looked back so fervently on his past was at a Glam Slam greatest hits gig in 1993, which is what portions of Tuesday's concert were most reminiscent of. After that Glam Show show, Prince went full bore into a creative period that produced such good-to-great new works as *Come, The Gold Experience, Emancipation,* and *The Truth.*

More good news: after he quit baseball, Jordan went on to win three rings. ■

VH1's Best Album Series Celebrates Prince's Classic *Purple Rain* Tonight

January 18, 2001

ON THE NIGHT OF AUGUST 3, 1983, PRINCE AND HIS NEW band, the Revolution, took the stage at a jam-packed First Avenue nightclub in downtown Minneapolis. It was guitarist Wendy Melvoin's first gig with the band, which was performing a benefit for the Minnesota Dance Theater at the behest of its founder, Loyce Houlton.

In the crowd that night was Chrissie Dunlap, who booked bands at First Avenue and was in those days a full-blown Prince fanatic. "It was the best Prince concert I ever saw," said

Dunlap, who attended all of Prince's surprise concerts at First Avenue throughout the '80s. "It was the first time we'd heard any of those songs, and he was on fire that night. He was at his peak."

In addition to being an unforgettable (and much boot-legged) live performance, the seventy-minute show was significant, for it planted the seeds for *Purple Rain*, which a panel of VH1-polled experts recently named the eighteenth greatest rock 'n' roll album of all time. Six new songs saw their debut that night, five of which ended up on *Purple Rain*. The entire concert was recorded in a mobile unit by engineers David Leonard and David Rivkin, and the basic tracks for three songs culled from the set ("I Would Die 4 U," "Baby I'm a Star," and "Purple Rain") were used on the album.

"It's one of my top five concerts of all time," says veteran critic and Prince watcher P. D. Larson. "It was hot—literally and figuratively. It was the first time anyone heard 'Purple Rain,' which has become sort of the 'Stairway to Heaven' of its time. I remember he wore that huge hoop earring, and all those new songs just had an immediate impact. They obviously felt the same way, like they couldn't re-create them, because they ended up on the album."

"Certainly," writes former Prince manager Alan Leeds, in the liner notes to *The Hits/The B-Sides*, "none of us had an inkling that those very performances, with only minimal studio alterations, would help define pop music in the coming year."

Other than the erotic fantasy "Darling Nikki," which Prince recorded in his home studio in Chanhassen, and "Let's Go Crazy," which was recorded at the band's rehearsal space in St. Louis Park, much of the album was recorded in Studio 3 in Sunset Sound Studios in Los Angeles. In Per Nilsen's book *Dance Music Sex Romance: Prince—The First Decade,* Prince's engineer, Peggy McCreary, recalls, "Studio 3 was like a womb that wrapped around you for protection. We had a bathroom, a kitchen, and we would shut ourselves off from everything. We

didn't need to go out because the studio was a separate building. He wanted to use strings and all kinds of things. I said,
'Excuse me, we only have 24-track machines. We don't have
enough room.' And he just said, 'Make some more room.' That's
just the way he works. So I had to hook up two tape machines."

The sessions were attended by most of the Revolution, and
Prince's close friends Jill Jones and Susannah Melvoin. The
liner notes have it as "produced, arranged, composed and performed by Prince and the Revolution," but, as has usually been
the case with Prince, the making of *Purple Rain* was mostly a
one-man show.

It was also arguably Prince's most prolific period, and as-
toundingly so: in addition to laying down all the *Purple Rain*
material and B-sides ("17 Days," "Erotic City," "She's Always in
My Hair," "God," "Another Lonely Christmas"), the sessions
yielded material for his next album, *Around the World in a Day,*
the Time album *Ice Cream Castles,* Apollonia 6's debut album,
and Sheila E.'s debut album, *The Glamorous Life.*

When the entire *Purple Rain* album was completed, however, Prince went back into Sunset Sound to record two new
songs—"Take Me with U" and "When Doves Cry," which became Prince's first No. 1 single, and the first single in history
that didn't rely on a bass line for its groove. "He started the
song the way he always did, with a drum machine," McCreary
told Nilsen. "Then he added bass and synths, then this and
that. Something was bothering him about it, but he couldn't
put his finger on it at first. Finally, he reached over and punched
out the bass track. That's when we knew we had something
special. He said something like, 'Nobody would have the balls
to do this. You just wait, they'll be freaking.' He knew exactly
what he was doing . . . and just knew he had a hit. It was just
the two of us in the studio. It was a really quiet time, a very personal time in the studio, and I think it was at times like that
that he made his best music."

The *Purple Rain* album was completed in April 1984 and released in June. The film, which was shot mostly in November and December 1983, premiered in July. The movie became
a critical and commercial blockbuster; the album topped the
album charts for six months and yielded several chart-top-
ping singles. Save for some new-waveish production tics and
echo-saturated vocals, the record stands the test of time. The
songs are written from, but not limited to, the viewpoint of
the movie's character, the Kid, and can be heard as one man's
exploration of the sacred and the profane, spirit and sexuality,
soul and flesh. It was a bracing paean to positivity, and for all
the discussion of the bass-lessness of "When Doves Cry," that
track also includes one of rock's most sublime headphone moments, when careful listeners can hear Prince snap his fingers
spontaneously after singing the first line, "Dig, if you will, the
picture of you and I engaged in a kiss."

There are many other high points, especially the impossi-
bly euphoric "Let's Go Crazy" and some of Prince's most in-
cendiary guitar work, all of which led the *Village Voice* to
dub him "the greatest rock-and-roll musician of the era—as
singer-guitarist-hooksmith-beatmaster, he has no peer."

In June 1985, Prince held a party for himself at the Prom
Center in St. Paul. His birthday celebration has become something of a tradition, but this one was especially memorable because it marked the culmination of a two-year period that saw
him transform from cult artist into the biggest pop star in the
world. "It was a costume ball, a totally surreal scene," Larson
says. "Pee-wee Herman was walking around, and it was the first
time I'd ever seen Hollywood-style paparazzi. The food, drinks,
and whole layout [were] incredible, and the band jammed on
a few songs, which was cool. At about 3 A.M., I went out to get
some air. And Prince was standing there by his white Thunderbird, surrounded by a mob of kids from the neighborhood who
had seen what was happening on the 10 o'clock news and came

down. He was signing autographs and hanging out with these kids from the Frogtown neighborhood.

"He had a really bad public image at this point, and I always thought that it was a cool little scene to happen upon, because here he was, king of the world, no bodyguards or anything around, just chilling with these kids. Part of me thought that he was thinking, 'Hey, this could have been me, fifteen years ago.'" ■

For Prince, It's All about Sex, God, and Rock 'n' Roll

June 15, 2001

WHY HAS THE NEWS THAT PRINCE HAS EMBRACED THE faith of the Jehovah's Witnesses been met with so much suspicion? Why should such a revelation surprise anyone, coming as it does from a man who has spent most of his forty-three years, and his entire recording career, celebrating God?

Maybe because it is the Big Unspeakable in the media and in polite society in general, because—thanks to right wingers and other God cops—to reveal such a personal relationship is to be in cahoots with nutcases, extremists, and zealots. But one man's cult is another man's church, and the fact remains that the B-side to Prince's most famous single, "Purple Rain," was "God." Furthermore, one of his best-ever songs, the one that gets played in basketball arenas and on radio stations all over the world, kicks off with a vocal that sounds as if it were recorded in the Grand Canyon, and as if it belonged not to a pop star but to a preacher: "Dearly beloved, we are gathered here to get through this thing called life."

Which is what Prince, like the rest of us, has been doing all these years—getting through this thing called life. To many, his public persona is that of control freak, media manipulator, and/or sexy mofo, but where it counts—in the grooves—the little man has always been asking big questions. And the one constant to his search has been his faith, which he has sung about on every record he has released, in songs such as "The Holy River," "The Cross," "Gold," "I Wish U Heaven," "God's Spirit," "And God Created Woman," "Thieves in the Temple," "The Work," "Anna Stesia," "The Truth," "Annie Christian," "The Ladder," "Mountains," "Soul Sanctuary," "Spirit," "Gold," "Count the Days," "Into the Light," and, yes, "My Name Is Prince." Among many others.

So what's the big deal? I mean, in the middle of "Controversy," for heaven's sakes, he recited part of the Lord's Prayer. One of his most memorable covers was Joan Osborne's "One of Us," for which he changed the lyrics to "Just a *slave* like one of us?" And the easiest way to find Paisley Park at night is to look for the glowing peace symbol that rests atop the studio's highest spire and cuts the Chanhassen sky like a beacon.

The truth is, Prince has done more in the name of love/God than many do-gooders who ostensibly give their lives to one religion or another. And it is hilariously ironic that conservative Christians regularly come out against Prince, or burn his records, because it's obvious that they've got dogma in their ears.

That, or sex makes them nervous. Or they don't consider sex to be God's work, but I do. Call me Jimmy the Blasphemer, but I'm here to say that when Prince sings about getting nasty, he's also singing about getting right with God, whether it's "Head," "Erotic City," "Sex in the Summer," "Housequake," "Hot Wit U," "Pink Cashmere," "Gett Off," "Insatiable," "Shhh," or "Pussy Control." Among many others.

And he's always, always, always singing about love. Which, again, is to say that he's singing about God, as he does on such love celebrations as "Live 4 Love," "Love for One Another,"

"Boys and Girls," "Love . . . Thy Will Be Done," "Noon Rendez-vous," "Adore," "I Love U in Me," "Eye Hate U," "When 2 R in Love," or "I Wanna Be Your Lover." Among many others.

Then there's the music itself—magnificent, miraculous, merciless bass-bumped funk—which is arguably the most Godlike music ever created because it fuses the torso with the head, heart, and soul like nothing else. And it occurs to me that by doing so, by getting us to dance, Prince isn't necessarily preaching about what he's found specifically so much as encouraging us to find what works for us, and to believe in something bigger than ourselves, be it Jesus, Jah, Jehovah, or Jolt.

Which is what happens to most musicians somewhere along the way. Most musicians, if they don't start out believing in God, end up doing so, because after a while they can't believe themselves, or what they've done. There are countless examples of musicians saying, "That wasn't me. That song just happened. I didn't write that, it came to me in a dream, fully formed." In doing so, they both embrace and distance themselves from their gift—a necessary survival tactic, because its power to move souls is so profound. And, for the gifted one, often overwhelming.

Last summer around this time, I hung out with Prince and his bass player, Larry Graham, for a couple of hours in Prince's office at Paisley Park. Prince had asked me to come out to the studio to discuss a column I wrote, an open letter in which I requested of him one more "great record." I expounded on my need for him to be a big star again, to reclaim his throne and to kick all the bad music off the airwaves. He couldn't have cared less about my version of success, or what I thought the world needed from him. He said, "I've been to the top of the mountain, and there was nothing there."

So he found something. He told me about it, as he scrolled through the text of my column on his computer, reading almost every line out loud, laughing, challenging, questioning. When he got to the bit where I'd written, "Several lesser lights have made off with your crown because you've been distracted by the task at hand (making music that describes right now) by music industry–grousing, name changes, cryptic religious questions but no answers," he stopped. He smirked and raised his eyebrows at me. At the time, I saw those eyebrows as a condescending expression of the know-it-all nouveau religious. But I've since come to the conclusion that they were saying two things: "The answers are out there" and "No one but you can provide you with the answers you need."

He's right, of course. Everyone's answers are different, because everyone's questions are different. And Prince—who has lived one of the weirder lives known to man or God, starting with the fact that he comes from a broken home and grew up a black genius in mostly white Minnesota—has found some answers and some peace, and I for one am happy for him.

Tonight and Saturday, he'll continue his continuing question-answer session at the Xcel Energy Center, as well as on his forthcoming album, *The Rainbow Children*. About which I have a very good feeling, by the way, because I have faith, as Prince's soul brother Terence Trent D'Arby once sang, in these desolate times. ∎

(Another) Open Letter to Prince

June 20, 2002

DEAR PRINCE,
I owe you a letter. Been a while. Two years, almost exactly, since I wrote you on the eve of the first Prince: A Celebration and challenged you to make another great record. I asked, "What are we celebrating?" Remember? I do.

I remember plenty of things these days, these crazy scary precious days, as you and your "fam" gear up for your latest summer celebration, Xenophobia. I remember the first time I saw you in concert—at Sam's, before it was First Avenue, the night before you went to Los Angeles and got booed off the stage opening for the Rolling Stones. It was 1981, nobody cared much about the Twin Cities, the concept of regional music scenes had faded, and then along you came with your garter belts and your Telecaster and your dirty mind and all your nude ambition.

I remember "Pink Cashmere." "Alone One Night." "When Doves Cry." "Sex in the Summer." "Take Me with U." "Manic Monday." "Don't Play Me." "Girls and Boys." I remember "Chloreen Bacon Skin," which everyone who thinks I write about you too much should hear, because if they haven't, then they haven't heard you, and they are lucky if they are an iota this free or funky.

I remember the summer of *Purple Rain*. I remember what First Avenue's Chrissie Dunlap told me for an article I did for *SPIN* on the Twin Cities scene: "It just exploded. It was so alive. It was the center of everything. These bands started getting national attention, and all of a sudden we felt sort of important and like we mattered. It was a novel thing for Minneapolis, because the coasts had always been the cool places. I just felt terribly proud of my bands and my club and my city. It was almost a little magical."

I remember standing in front of your piano at Paisley Park when you played "The Most Beautiful Girl in the World" for the first time. I remember standing in front of the stage in the old upper annex of Glam Slam while you lay on your back, lost in a twenty-minute blues jam. I remember many mornings, walking out of Paisley Park with the birds chirping and the sun coming up over Chanhassen. I remember driving home and searching for adjectives to describe what I'd just witnessed.

I remember where I was and the Uptown Girl I was with and how our jaws dropped when we saw Gene Siskel and Roger

Ebert thumbs-up your first movie. I remember standing in front of the stage at a gig by you and the *Sign o' the Times* band at First Avenue. I remember seeing you and the Revolution at First Avenue the week *Purple Rain* hit theaters and record stores, and, damn right, I am bragging.

Everybody who has stories like those brags, because Chrissie is right: Brother, you made us proud. You blew our minds. You told the world about this beautiful place you still call Uptown. You raised our spirits when they were down, because the '80s were as much of a drag as the '00s are getting to be. Politicians were talkin' loud and sayin' nothing, and money was everything, and you couldn't believe in anything, and there you were, singing about what everyone was talking about. Love, race, community, spirituality, sex.

I remember last Friday, when I took the bus to Walker Art Center's free Rock the Garden festival. It was an idyllic night, the sun was hanging low over the Cherry Spoon, which sprayed a mist over the Sculpture Garden's lush green everything and its multiculti citizens. The music—Iffy, Marc Ribot & Los Cubanos Postizos, Medeski Martin & Wood—was as delicious as the people watching. I walked home afterward and thought about how much you would have loved it. It reminded me of the utopia you've sung about so often. Black, white, Puerto Rican, African, and Irish American, everybody all a-freakin'.

I remember early mornings in the early '80s, working at D. B. Kaplan's, a deli in Butler Square in downtown Minneapolis. Most of the kids who worked there were musicians, poets, actors, writers, students. We sliced meat and cheese and waited tables and tended bar and survived manic breakfast, lunch, and dinner rushes and talked about our parents, politics, futures.

Everybody was basically sleeping with everybody else and listening to you. We remember "Controversy." "1999." "When U Were Mine." "Purple Rain."

I remember in those days how people from all over the world would flock to First Avenue and have their pictures taken in front of it, just as they will this week. Friday night, the lit-up red letters on the Orpheum Theatre marquee will scream "Prince," which is another way of screaming "possibility," which is why, at the moment, I've got a better question than the one I asked two years ago:

How could I forget? ■

Jim Walsh is an award-winning journalist and songwriter from Minneapolis. A columnist for the *Southwest Journal,* his writing has appeared in *Rolling Stone,* the *Village Voice,* the *St. Paul Pioneer Press, City Pages,* Minnpost.com, and many other publications. He is the author of *Bar Yarns and Manic-Depressive Mixtapes: Jim Walsh on Music from Minneapolis to the Outer Limits* (Minnesota, 2016); *The Replacements: All Over but the Shouting: An Oral History*; and, with Dennis Pernu, *The Replacements: Waxed Up Hair and Painted Shoes: The Photographic History*. He is the former leader of the bands REMs, Laughing Stock, and the Mad Ripple and the ringleader behind the singer/songwriter showcase the Mad Ripple Hootenanny.